DEGREES OF CHOICE
Class, race, gender and higher education

*Diane Reay, Miriam E. David
and Stephen Ball*

Trentham Books
Stoke on Trent, UK and Sterling, USA

Trentham Books Limited

Westview House	22883 Quicksilver Drive
734 London Road	Sterling
Oakhill	VA 20166-2012
Stoke on Trent	USA
Staffordshire	
England ST4 5NP	

First published 2005

Reprinted 2009

British Library Cataloguing-in-Publication Data
A catalogue record for this book is available from the
British Library

ISBN-13: 978-1-85856-330-5
ISBN-10: 1-85856-330-5

Designed and typeset by Trentham Print Design Ltd., Chester
and printed in Great Britain by Cpod, a division of The Cromwell Press Group,
Trowbridge, Wiltshire

Contents

Acknowledgements

We would all like to thank Jacqueline Davies who did a sterling job in relation to the project, especially the quantitive data analysis.

Diane would like to thank Linsey Reay, Jamie Reay, Julian Meteyard, Kuval Sutton-Patel and Maya Sutton-Patel for nurturing and sustaining her non-academic self and always providing a different perspective.

Miriam would like to thank Charlotte Reiner, Toby Reiner and Jeff Duckett for providing the rationale for the study and yet maintaining a healthy and sceptical perspective.

Introduction

'Class gap widens under Blair' was the headline in the *Times Higher Education Supplement* of July 2 2004, despite policies on widening participation and access to higher education. The Higher's editorial (*ibid*, p12) went on to condemn the class divisions opening up in higher education. This book addresses such concerns around growing inequalities in higher education. The rhetoric of the New Labour Government in the UK celebrates the widening of access and the essential fairness of the meritocratic principle. We want to problematise such comforting notions by showing how the welcome expansion of higher education has been accompanied by a deepening of educational and social stratification and the emergence of new forms of inequality. We have found that young and mature, male and female students confront very differing degrees of choice and these are significantly shaped by their social class.

So the main aim of our book is to draw attention to the need to take seriously the issue of who goes where and who does what in higher education. It is not that the issue of who gets in is any less important but rather that the move to a mass system of higher education means it is increasingly important that we consider the different sorts of higher educations that are now on offer. We may have a mass system of higher education in the twenty-first century but it is neither equal nor common for all.

Our secondary aim is to develop a sociology of higher education choice by bringing to life the diverse voices and experiences of young and mature, male and female students in an analysis that draws on Pierre Bourdieu's concepts of habitus, field and cultural capital. The area of higher education choice is both under-researched and under-theorised. A number of influential books and articles have been written that examine choice of nursery or primary school (West *et al*, 1998, Vincent *et al*, 2004), secondary school (David *et al*, 1994, Gewirtz *et al*, 1995) and Further Education (FE) (Ball, *et al*, 2000; Foskett and Hemsley-Brown, 2001).

These are mainly from the perspective of parents and families rather than the young people themselves. Very little exists in the UK, the US or Australia that theorises issues of both choice and access in relation to higher education apart from Archer, Hutchings and Ross' (2003) work based on London Metropolitan University and McDonough's (1997) study of choice making in four US high schools. Drawing on Bourdieu's work on distinction and judgement, we take the concept of habitus and the development of the concept to include institutional and familial habitus and use them to understand and explain the choices students make of higher education. Our aim is to link school (institutional habitus) and family (class habitus) with individual choice-making and the workings of cultural capital in a sociologically informed dynamic. We argue that the perceptions, distinctions and choices of higher education institutions used and made by students play a part in reconstituting and reproducing the divisions and hierarchies in higher education.

In particular, the book's deliberate focus on non-traditional students – working class, ethnic minority, and mature women as well as white, middle class female and male applicants – allows for an in-depth engagement with topical policy issues around widening access and equity in relation to higher education. The narratives of prospective male and female students in higher education bring to life the contradictions and difficulties arising from attempts to expand student numbers at a time when higher education funding is under increasing pressure. As Coffield and Vignoles (1997) succinctly state, 'the higher education system in the UK is mass in size but still elite in its values, over crowded and under funded'.

Our first two chapters set the scene for the empirical study. The first part of chapter one examines the recent history and demography of higher education. The higher education (HE) system has undergone massive change in the past 20 years. This includes growth in the participation rate from 12 per cent to a current rate of 44 per cent with a target of 50 per cent by 2010. The changing gender balance of both full-time and part-time students is a major phenomenon of this period, across social class and mode of study.

A significant proportion of this expansion of higher education is made up of redefining or including activities not before considered as or counted as higher education. For example, certain subjects like teacher education and para-medical professional education have been included in higher education especially universities, when previously they were not considered suitable subjects for study at this level. This accounts for some of the changing gender balance and yet the shift in other vocational subjects also alters the nature and forms of higher education in more complex ways. We describe these changes and their implications for higher education access and participation, particularly in relation to social class, but also in relation to gender and ethnicity. The second part of the chapter introduces both the quantitative and qualitative study samples on which the research is based and the six educational institutions in which the research is set.

Chapter two then sets out the theoretical framework for examining the notion of choice of higher education in the rest of the book. We examine higher education choice through the lens of Bourdieu's theoretical framework and so in the first part of the chapter the utility of Bourdieu's concepts of habitus, cultural capital and field is discussed. The second part of chapter two begins to examine the use of Bourdieu's concepts and shows how habitus as 'the practical mastery people possess of their situations' (Robbins, 1991, p1) and cultural capital as 'subtle modalities in the relationship to culture and language' (Bourdieu, 1977, p82) are at work in the decisions higher education applicants make.

Chapter three examines the idea of the 'school effect' by utilising the concept of institutional habitus in order to explore the impact made by individual institutions on the attainment of prospective university applicants and their subsequent destinations within higher education. In spite of an inevitable degree of overlap and blurring of boundaries between peer group, family and institution the case is made that there are specific effects which derive from attending a particular educational institution. These become most evident when examining the choices of similar kinds of students across the private-state divide. In chapter four we explore the closely related notion of parental involvement in student choices of higher education, focusing on the ways in which families and especially parents are involved in the processes of decision making about higher education. The concept of familial habitus is utilised to explore how differences in cultural, economic, social and academic capital impact on higher education choices.

Some recent statistics suggest that the policy changes have made it more rather than less difficult for non-traditional students, especially women, to attend university (Callender 2003a; Callender and Kemp, 2000). Chapter five explores the sociological and psychological processes which make working class transitions to higher education problematic by focusing on the narratives of working class young and mature but mainly female students. Many of the working class students in the sample were access students attending an FE college where the balance was tipped in favour of mature women students, but the chapter also examines the accounts of the small number of young working class students taking the more traditional A level route. The chapter also demonstrates how while class always counts in the transition process, it is always mediated by gender and ethnicity. There is no uniformity of class conditions, practices and outcomes, but rather, different working class fractions with differing priorities in relation to risk, challenge and fitting in.

Chapter six moves on to focus on the analysis of over half our sample, namely a sub-sample of 65 ethnic minority students, again where there were slightly more women than men. Ethnic mix is examined and discussed in relation to ethnic identity. The chapter concentrates on two key findings. First, the processes, concerns, resources and outcomes of choosing differ among the ethnic minority students in relation to social class. Class differences are more apparent and significant than ethnic minority differences. Second, for a large minority of these students, 25 out of the 65, the ethnic mix of higher education institutions is one factor, among others, that influences their choice.

In chapter seven we consider the information, both formal and informal, that higher education applicants use in their decision making. In order fully to understand the information processing students and their families engage in, the marketing strategies of higher education providers are discussed. However, the main focus of the chapter is the practices of applicants, the tactics they employ, their readings and mis-readings of universities, and the social differences and divisions that result from the enormously varied quantity and quality of social, cultural and economic capital among the sample. The dominant model of decision making is still that of rational choice theory in which students are perceived to be economic decision-makers. However, our data, particularly those from in-depth qualitative interviews, indicate that decision making is often a messy process in which intuition, affective response and serendipity can play a greater role than rational calculation and systematic evaluation of the evidence available.

Finally Chapter 8 provides a concise overview of the book as a whole, re-articulating the classed, gendered and racialised nature of both higher education decision making and higher education institutions. We discuss the implications of the study for the field of higher education and for the future direction of policy. We conclude that issues of social justice and equity are key to policy in relation to higher education choice and discuss the importance of making both central to provision and policy.

1

Setting the scene

Section 1: The Changing Demographics of HE

Egerton and Halsey (1993) identify three major aspects of the history of access to higher education over the twentieth century. Firstly, it has been a period of considerable expansion, secondly, there has been a significant reduction in gender inequality and thirdly, there has been no reduction in relative social class inequality. Before the second world war university education was the preserve of a small elite. In 1938 less than 2 per cent of the relevant age cohort were attending universities and among women the percentage was less than 0.5 (Blackburn and Jarman, 1993). By 1948 the proportion of the eighteen year old population entering universities was still only 3.7. However, while the proportion of women attending universities has slowly risen over the post war period until it has now overtaken that of men (Arnot *et al*, 1999), social class differences in access have remained far more intractable.

From 1928 to 1947 8.9 per cent of all boys from non-manual backgrounds entered university compared to 1.4 per cent of all boys from manual backgrounds (Glass, 1954). Halsey *et al*'s (1980) comparison of access trends before and after the war suggest that the immediate post-war situation had become even more skewed in class terms than that existing before the war. However, the introduction of means tested grants and the provision of full fees in

1960 (Anderson, 1960), plus the Robbins Report's (1963) endorsement of the principle that university education should be available to all those with the ability and qualifications to benefit provided the policy background for a rapid expansion. As a consequence there was a rise of 50 per cent in university entrance between 1963 and 1968. Although the Anderson and Robbins policies were followed by a decline in class inequalities, from 1970 to 1980 there was an increase in inequality as class advantage proved crucial in the heightened competition resulting from the growth in demand perpetuated by economic and labour market changes. Between 1970 and 1989 the number of university entrants rose by 150 per cent. Yet despite this enormous growth, class differentials in higher education have remained fairly constant (Blackburn and Jarman, 1993; Gillon, 1999). Just as Bourdieu and Passeron (1979) found in the French university sector, there is a persistent over-representation of middle class students.

By 1996, the first-time participation rates in higher education in the UK had exceeded 33 per cent[1]. This is an enormous shift since the 1960s when rates were below 10 per cent (OECD, 1998). This expansion of higher education entailed changes in the characteristics of institutions and their student clientele. In the UK, over the last twenty five years, there has been a massive increase in the numbers of students participating in higher education, from three quarters of a million students to well over two million. This has also entailed a dramatic shift in the balance between male and female students. In 1975-6 the ratio of female to male students – the gender gap – was 0.46:1 whereas by 1999-2000 this had reversed to 1.20:1 for all full and part-time students (1.15:1 for full-time students and 1.28:1 for part-time students). Similarly there has been an enormous increase in the proportions of students obtaining the necessary qualifications to enter higher education, with a similar transformation in the gender gap from 0.85:1 to 1.21:1 over the same period. As Tables 1 and 2 below show, the proportion of pupils in the United Kingdom gaining two or more GCE A levels (or equivalent) has increased from 30 per cent in 1995/96 to 39 per cent in 2001/02. The proportion of young women who achieve this has increased from 20 per cent in 1992/93 to 43 per cent in 2001/02. For young men over the same period, the increase has been

Table 1: Achievement at GCE A level[1] or equivalent
United Kingdom

Percentages

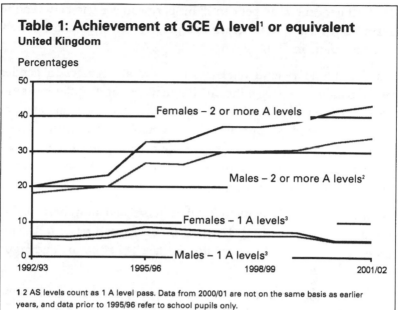

1 2 AS levels count as 1 A level pass. Data from 2000/01 are not on the same basis as earlier years, and data prior to 1995/96 refer to school pupils only.
2 Equivalent to 3 or more Highers.
3 Equivalent to 1 or 2 Highers. Includes those with 1.5 A levels.

Source: Department for Education and Skills; National Assembly for Wales; Scottish Executive; Northern Ireland Department of Education

Table 2: Achievement at GCE A level[1] or equivalent

United Kingdom				Percentages
	Males		Females	
	2 or more A levels[2]	1 A level[3]	2 or more A levels[2]	1 A level[3]
1992/93	18.3	5.0	20.1	5.8
1993/94	19.1	4.9	21.9	5.8
1994/95	20.0	5.4	23.1	6.7
1995/96	26.7	7.1	32.7	8.6
1996/97	26.5	6.7	33.0	8.1
1997/98	29.9	6.0	37.4	7.2
1998/99	30.1	6.1	37.4	7.3
1999/2000	30.5	6.0	38.6	7.1
2000/01	32.9	4.5	41.7	4.9
2001/02	34.1	4.4	43.2	4.8

1 2 AS levels count as 1 A level pass. Data from 2000/01 are not on the same basis as earlier years, and data prior to 1995/96 refer to school pupils only.
2 Equivalent to 3 or more Highers.
3 Equivalent to 1 or 2 Highers. Includes those with 1.5 A levels.

Source: Department for Education and Skills; National Assembly for Wales; Scottish Executive; Northern Ireland Department of Education

from 18 per cent to 34 per cent. This performance gap between the sexes has widened to 9 percentage points, from just under 2 percentage points in 1992/ 93.

But we should remind ourselves that overall changes in gender participation mark significant inequalities and differences in gender participation in different subject areas. Gender inequalities are still very evident, mirroring the inequalities in A levels, where boys predominate in physics, mathematics, computer studies, technology and economics and more girls choose biology, social studies and art and design (Arnot et al, 1999).

By the end of the twentieth century there had only been a tiny decline in class inequality. Blackburn and Jarman point to the increasing significance of universities in the class structure and argue that:

> Central to this change is the way university degrees have become so much more important as criteria for job placement. When degrees were held by less than 2 per cent of the labour force, they may have been extremely important for the careers of the qualified men and women but they were too rare to have a major impact on the labour market as a whole. As the number of graduates has grown the degree has become an increasingly common entry qualification for a growing number of high-level occupations. Thus higher education has played a progressively greater part in the reproduction of the occupationally based class structure. So it is not surprising that class inequalities have persisted. Nor is it surprising that class differentials among women are just as marked as they are among men. (Blackburn and Jarman, 1993: 205)

The situation throughout the twentieth century, then, has been one of a strong class differential among both men and women in which social class effects have neither been alleviated nor accentuated by gender (Egerton and Halsey, 1993; Halsey, 1993). However, gender does have other effects. Women benefit less from a degree in terms of labour market participation. For example women graduates have average earnings lower than male graduates in all major occupational groups (Purcell, 2002).

As Lesley Pugsley points out, 'there are class inequalities involved in making decisions about higher education which have persisted for the 40 years since Jackson and Marsden's 1962 study' (1998, p85). And, significantly, this is not simply a reflection of class differences in prior educational attainment. The differences in class recruitment to higher education persist even when entry requirements are taken into account. Data from the Youth Cohort survey of 1993 found that while 77 per cent of children from social classes 1 and 2 with two A levels or equivalent went on to higher education, the proportion for social classes 4 and 5 was only 47 per cent (Metcalf, 1997). Furthermore, policy changes initiated in 1997 have made it more, not less, difficult for young people from lower social classes to attend university and this is borne out by the statistics:

> Analysis of 1997 to 1998 data highlight large decreases in accepted applicants within those age, socio-economic and ethnic groupings which were the primary focus of the widening participation initiative. (UCAS, 2000: 8)

Rachel Brooks (2004) argues that, since the late 1990s, although widening participation remains a central plank in the government's higher education policy, its impact to date in terms of equity appears negligible. Rather, the inequalities arising from lack of information and general perplexity and confusion about post-compulsory education which existed among Jackson and Marsden's working class families of forty years ago have, in the new Labour era, been compounded by the introduction of fees and loans and the abolition of maintenance grants.

Since Jackson and Marsden's study (1962) the class landscape of Britain has changed radically. The old binary between working and middle class has never explained enough about the myriad ways in which social class is acted out in people's lives. Even Jackson and Marsden wrote about different groupings within their working class category. Thirty-eight per cent of their working class sample were described as 'sunken middle class'. Similarly, current research indicates that it is important to disaggregate crude class categorisations and develop more subtle analyses which recognise rather than gloss over increasing horizontal and vertical segmentation within class groupings (Savage et al, 1992; Savage, 2000; Power et al, 2003).

While the increasing complexities of class positionings signal the need for more sophisticated, nuanced analyses, it is important still to recognise enduring class inequalities. In 1998 the class participation rate of the three lowest social classes had fallen from 22.1 in 1997 to 21.3 per cent, while the class participation rate for social classes 1, 2 and 3N rose from 51.8 to 55.8 per cent (Gillon, 1999). Since 1998 participation rates have increased more rapidly among the middle classes than the working classes (Galindo-Rueda *et al*, 2004). One of Galindo-Rueda *et al*'s (2004) more stark findings was that the difference between proportions of middle class and working class children going to university almost doubled between 1994-5 and 2001-2. They argue that if you examine what is happening at the very top and bottom of the socio-economic scale in particular, the situation is dire. Almost 80 per cent of students from professional backgrounds study for a degree, compared to just 15 per cent of those from unskilled backgrounds (see Table 3 opposite).

A significant minority of the working class students in our qualitative sample (nineteen out of 41) were mature students on access courses. It is important to chart the recent history of mature students within the field of higher education. Mature students were seen as playing a pivotal role in the 1987 Department of Education and Science plan for expansion and reform of the higher education system: *HE: Meeting the Challenge*. The stated objective was for universities to recruit more non-traditional students both in terms of age and entrance requirements. The social groups to be targeted were women, ethnic minorities, disabled and working class people, with access courses being officially designated as the third route into higher education (DES, 1987). By 1989 there were approximately 400 access courses in 50 local education authorities (LEAs), with 6,000 students in FE colleges (Smithers and Robins, 1995). The 1990s expansion of higher education was, in part, made possible by this initiative. Mature entry rose from approximately 10 per cent of all graduates and diploma holders in 1980 to over 30 per cent in 1990 (DFE, 1992). In 1994-5 15.7 per cent of first degree, full-time enrolments were age 25 or over. Of these 6.7 per cent were between 25 and 30, while 9 per cent were 30 or over (DFEE, 1996). Of the 500,000 part-time higher education enrol-

Table 3: Age Participation Index (API) (%) by social class, 1991/2-2001

Year of Entry	1992	1993	1994	1995	1996	1997	1998	1999	2000	2001
Class										
Professional (A)	71	73	78	80	82	79	72	73	76	79
Intermediate (B)	39	42	45	46	47	48	45	45	48	50
Skilled non-man (C1)	27	29	31	31	32	31	29	30	33	33
Skilled manual (C2)	15	17	18	18	18	19	18	18	19	21
Partly skilled (D)	14	16	17	17	17	18	17	17	19	18
Unskilled (E)	9	11	11	12	13	14	13	13	14	15
A-C1	40	43	46	47	48	48	45	45	48	50
C2-E	14	16	17	17	18	18	17	17	18	19

Source: Department for Education and Skills Age Participation Index which measures the proportion of the under 21s in each social class participating in Higher Education for the first time (i.e. young entrants from each social class as a percentage of all young people in each social class).

ments 80 per cent were aged 25 or over and 60 per cent of these were 30 or over.

More recent UCAS figures have shown a consistent decline in the number of applications of mature students entering higher education (O'Leary, 2000; UCAS, 2000). Recent statistics indicate the dramatic impact of the introduction of fees on the number of mature students entering UK universities (Major, 2000). In 1997-8 100,300 mature freshers started full-time undergraduate courses. In 1998-9 mature entrants numbered 90,585 – a fall of 10 per cent. Since 2000 there has been a slight improvement. However, the introduction of fees seems likely to have disproportionately affected non-traditional students. Muriel Egerton's profile of mature students, constructed using data from both the Labour Force Survey and the General Household Survey, shows only marginal change in the participation of the disadvantaged groups that the DES had proposed targeting (Egerton, 1999). The only exception she found was women whose participation rose to parity or more than parity both as young or mature students. Again nationally middle class mature students still outnumber their working class counterparts (Egerton and Halsey, 1993). More recent UK statistics paint an even more pessimistic picture of participation disparities despite an increasing emphasis on encouraging participation among working class groups (Connor et al, 1999; Hill, 2004). Policy changes initiated in 1997 seem to have made it more, not less, difficult for individuals from lower social classes to attend university.

Whilst there has been a preoccupation with gender and class within research into higher education access in the UK, the operations of race and ethnicity have been largely neglected. The work of Paul Taylor in the early 1990s emphasised dissimilarities in the experience of disadvantage across different ethnic minority groupings, whilst stressing the continuing importance of class and gender (Taylor, 1992). More recently a range of studies have emerged which focus on ethnicity (Bird, 1996; Modood and Shiner, 1994; Modood and Acland, 1998; Shiner and Modood, 2002). What these studies consistently stress is that, despite their less advantaged parental occupational profile, 'most ethnic minority groups are producing greater proportions of applications and admissions to higher education than the rest of the population' (Modood, 1998 p37).

However, the recent statistics for home students generate some cause for concern. Between 1997 and 1998 the majority of ethnic minority groups showed increases in applicants accepted for degree courses but there were a number which had declined. The white category fell by 3.37 per cent but Black Caribbean and Black African applicants fell by nearly twice as much; 6.01 and 6.75 per cent respectively. Also, as we suggest later, the aggregate patterns of entry of ethnic minority and class groups tell only part of the story of inequalities in higher education. Attention also needs to be given to the distribution of entries across institutions. Here evidence to date indicates a troubling racial divide between the old and new sectors of higher education (Mirza, 1995) in which students of Caribbean origin are overrepresented by 43 per cent in new universities, Asians by 162 per cent and Africans by 223 per cent. In fact with the exception of Chinese students, ethnic minority students are concentrated in the new universities (Shiner and Modood, 2002; Connor et al, 2004).

In contemporary Britain, with the transition from an elite to mass system, higher education is going through the process of increased stratification very like that which Bourdieu (1988) describes in relation to France. Instead of a system underpinned by relatively straightforward class-based inclusion and exclusion, we now have a far more differentiated field of higher education (Collins, 1999). There is a political rhetoric of widening access, achievement-for-all and meritocratic equalisation within mass higher education. Yet changes in the scale and scope of higher education, however significant these may be, should not distract attention from the continuing and developing forms of social stratification within higher education and thus in relation to labour market access and returns from investment in higher education. While more working class and ethnic minority students are entering university, for the most part they are entering different universities to their middle class counterparts. Furthermore the expansion of higher education has been of greatest benefit to the offspring of the middle classes. The class differentials in age-participation rates in higher education have increased (Gillon, 1999).

In the early twenty-first century there are reasons for both optimism and pessimism regarding greater equality in access to higher education. There has been an enormous expansion over the last decade, opening up higher education to groups of young and mature people who would not have previously considered doing a degree. At the same time, the ending of the binary divide in UK higher education, whilst negating traditional distinctions between institutions, has not resulted in equity between institutions. There is a clear hierarchy in which prestigious research universities have emerged as a top layer of elite institutions co-existing alongside a large group of recently designated universities which constitute a new layer of teaching-only institutions. And these elite universities remain overwhelmingly white and middle class in composition (HEFCE, 2000; Lampl, 2004). Furthermore, the abolition of maintenance grants and the introduction of fees and loans as a policy is still in its infancy and it remains to be seen if a sizeable proportion of students will be deterred from applying to higher education as a consequence and, if so, whether there will be a differential impact on the basis of gender, race or class. Recent research (Hesketh, 1999; Hutchings and Archer, 2001) suggests that students' financial experiences are shaped by a combination of cultural and economic capital, implicating both class and race.

It is against this background of national trends in relation to gender, race, class and higher education, an expanding mass higher education system and increasing differentiation within both the middle and working classes that our research has been conducted.

Section 2 The Research Study

Our research study was carried out from 1998 until 2000 and focuses upon two cohorts of student choosers, their parents and various intermediaries (careers teachers, sixth form tutors etc) in six educational institutions; an 11-18 mixed comprehensive with a large ethnic minority, working class intake (Creighton Community School – CCS) and a comprehensive sixth-form consortium which serves a socially diverse community (Maitland Union – MU), a tertiary college with a very large A-level population (Riverway College – RC), an FE College which runs HE Access courses (Fennister FE College – FFEC), and two prestigious private schools, one single-sex boys (Cosmopolitan Boys – CB), one single-sex girls (Hemsley Girls – HG). All the institutions are in or close to London. Our research is institutionally located in this way so that we can explore the effects of individual, familial and institutional influences and processes in choice-making. The extremely diverse nature of the institutions also allows us to examine the access and choice making processes for groups of students who differ in class background and ethnicity. But the research also has its limitations in terms of its particular location. In many ways London, with its heavy concentration of HEIs, is unique and stands out from the rest of the UK.

During the study we administered a questionnaire to 502 year 12 and 13 and FE students; ran focus groups and interviewed 120 students in depth. At first we interviewed those who had volunteered through the questionnaire, but we then attempted to broaden the sample to address imbalances, notably in relation to gender, and also to include a range of interesting cases, for example, first generation students and Oxbridge entrants in state schools. Of our 120 students, 65 were female and 55 male, 41 were from working class backgrounds (these students are the focus of chapter 5) and 65 from a wide range of ethnic minority backgrounds (the focus of chapter 6). Sixth form tutors and other key

Table 4: Summary of project data

	Questionnaires		Interviews completed		
	year13	year12	students	parents	key informants
FFEC	29		23	n/a	4
CB	44	26	13	4	2
HG	55	60	15	10	2
MU	67	57	33	14	3
RC	59	50	24	8	3
CCS	14*	41	12	4	1
	268	**234**	**120**	**40**	**15**

*The small number here reflects the size and nature of the sixth form and this is a type of institution we wanted to have represented in the study.

personnel were interviewed in all six institutions (fifteen in total), as were a sub-sample of forty parents of students in the study. Supplementing these three data sets were field notes from participant observation. We attended a range of events in all six institutions, including parents' evenings, higher education careers lessons, Oxbridge interview practice and tutor group sessions on the UCAS process.

The questionnaire survey provided contextual information and basic descriptive statistics of our sample, as well as help in selecting students for interview. All 502 questionnaires were analysed using SPSS. Our in-depth interviews elicited educational career histories from the students and a narrative account of their choice of higher education institutions. Specific questions were asked about information used, support received, constraints etc. We employed grounded coding techniques (Strauss, 1987) in our analysis of the interview data. The transcripts were open coded initially but as analysis proceeded, coding concentrated on the major emergent issues and allowed us to saturate our main hypothesis concerning the relationship between habituses and choice. As we discuss further in the next chapter, Bourdieu's three main concepts of habitus, field and cultural capital were all deployed in order to analyse sociologically the processes underpinning students' choice making practices. Work on developing the characteristics and dimensions of our primary codes was extended by using axial coding and constant comparison procedures. All the qualitative data was entered into Nudist, a qualitative data analysis package, which allowed us, using counts and searches, to verify or disconfirm the relevance of issues emerging through our manual coding. Nudist also allowed us to undertake a number of other frequency counts in relation to the interview data and was used throughout to search, sort and manage the data base.

As might be expected, the social class make up of the sample varies considerably between the institutions. This was an intention of our design, enabling us to look at the impact of familial and institutional habituses on choice-making of higher education. Over 80 per cent of the sample gave enough information to classify the occupation of the main earner; the mature FE students were classified by their own occupation.

%s Social class	CB	HG	RC	FFEC	MU	CCS
1-2	83	93	44	39	58	23
3nm	8	4	19	17	8	10
3m- 4-5	9	4	37	44	34	67

Table 5 Social Class of respondents by institution.

These class groupings, based on the Registrar General's classification of occupations, are quite differently related to other indicators; 68 (26%) of the sample had both parents with a degree, only five of these came from groups 3m, and 4-5; 41 had a father only with a degree, only five of these came from groups 3m, and 4-5; fourteen had a mother only with a degree, only one of these came from groups 3m, and 4-5. Thus, for those from whom we had complete information, over 75 per cent of middle class fathers, and less than 15 per cent of working class fathers had a degree or higher.[2] Given the way the information was elicited, the former probably underestimates and the latter over-estimates the actual percentages (50 per cent of the working class respondents did not answer this question). The percentage of university educated parents in our sample far outstrips the national average. In 1996 13 per cent of the adult population aged between 25 and 64 had degree level qualifications (OECD, 1998). By 2003 21 per cent of all people of working age in the UK had a degree (DfES, 2003).

In the rest of the book the term middle class refers to students from families in groups 1, 2 and 3 non manual; working class refers to students from families in groups 3m, 4 and 5, except in those cases where there appears to be more ambiguity about class positioning. In these cases we provide more detailed information including, where possible, actual parental occupations and type of housing. In later chapters we attempt to deconstruct both the middle and working class groupings for a more differentiated examination.

In addition to the traditional class categorisation outlined above we also constructed our own composite categorisation based on both parents' occupation, where present, and the parents' education.

It is this division of the middle classes into established, high earning and traditional middle class graduates that we draw on particularly in chapter 4, when we discuss parental involvement in higher education choice. We have similarly categorised our qualitative sample. In our qualitative sample we deliberately sought a different class profile to that of the quantitative sample. First, we included a far higher percentage of working class students (33%) than are to be found in the quantitative sample. Second, over 30 per cent of the qualitative sample were part of what we have termed the established middle classes. Although most of these students were located in the private sector, there was a significant minority in MU, only a handful in RC, none in CCS and one in FFEC. The rest of the qualitative sample was predominantly middle class traditional graduates (28%) with a sprinkling of the routine, non-manual A-level (intermediate) grouping (8%).

Table 6: Composite Class Categorisation by institution.

%s OVERALL	CB	HG	RC	FFEC	MU	CCS	
Social class							
Established, high earning occupations – PhDs	44	37	5	14	24	2	21%
Traditional middle class, graduates	27	48	19	21	25	11	28%
Intermediate routine non-manual, A-levels	10	10	20	10	11	7	12%
Skilled manual, shopworkers etc. some GCSEs	7	0	14	31	17	15	13%
Unskilled work, CSEs or less	1	0	7	14	4	2	4%
not working			1	7		2	1%
missing	10	4	33	7	19	62	21%

There are two important class divisions, at least, which constantly recur through our analysis and discussion. One, fairly obvious and almost always clear-cut, is between middle class and working class choosers, although here and generally through the text, the category middle class refers in the main to the 'service class'. As Goldthorpe (1995 p314) makes clear; 'the service class is a class of employees'. The main problem of demarcation is that of distinguishing them from other sorts of employees. There are two elements to this: first, benefits of employment over and above salary – that is, pension rights, increments, employment security and career opportunities; second, some degree of professional autonomy and managerial or administrative authority. Despite on-going changes in the labour market, these criteria do still provide a fairly robust basis for distinguishing service class employees from other middle class groups, specifically the intermediate middle class. That is, those employed in routine, low-autonomy, white-collar jobs.

The second class division highlights a set of more subtle and complex fractional differences within the middle class, and indeed more precisely within the service class. Intra-class differences are based upon family history, capitals, skills and dispositions. Differences between those families well established within the middle class with either or both high incomes and high volumes of relevant social capital and those with a shorter family history of middle classness and with lower incomes and lower but not insignificant levels of relevant cultural capital. The former (parents and children) are over-represented in private schools, and in Oxbridge attendance and are highly-credentialled. The latter (parents and children) are concentrated more in state schools and are less likely to have had family members who attended Oxbridge (or other elite Universities like Bristol and Durham). These fractions only map loosely onto what are sometimes called the old and new middle class and do not carry all of the connotations of Bernstein's (1996) use of these terms for example. For clarity, and to avoid confusion, we shall refer to the former as the established middle class and the latter as the novitiate middle class – perhaps not ideal terminology, but effective. The differences involved here are the specific focus of chapter 4.

Throughout the text, then, we write generically about the middle class in terms of aspects of choice which they have in common, and these are numerous and significant. Where differences within are important, we signal these and give examples from the families in our sample, and indeed on occasion point to the specific situation of some of the small number of intermediate middle class families in our sample. In chapter 5 we point to some differences within our working class sample and in chapter 6 we cross-cut class with ethnicity.

However, despite our attention to positional aspects of class, we subscribe to the new developing sociology of social class that focuses as much on class processes and practices as on position in the labour market (Savage, 2003; Skeggs, 2004). Much of the analysis that follows emphasises how applicants think, feel, act, judge, discern and prioritise in relation to higher education. This array of predispositions, dispositions and actions is frequently read through a classed lens in our analysis. We are looking for, and identifying class, in practices and collective social processes (Skeggs, 2004). Although we are working with what are, in effect, notions of an upper, middle and lower middle, as well as a working, class, based on educational background and occupation, we would caution that such simplistic divisions convey only a fraction of the story of social class. Rather, we try, through our qualitative data, to tell a more nuanced inflected tale. As Wacquant (1991: 52) argues in relation to the middle classes:

> The nature, composition and dispositions of the middle classes cannot be 'directly' deduced from an objectivist map of the social structure. Rather, they must be discovered through an analysis of the whole set of creative strategies of distinction, reproduction and subversion of all agents.

So our shorthand division of the qualitative sample, particularly in relation to an upper, middle and lower middle class, are further overlaid by attempts to read class in a range of practices of distinction and reproduction. These focus as much on affective responses to the higher education choice process, such as a sense of security or insecurity, familiarity or unfamiliarity, and attitudes and inclinations, such as solidarist or individualist tendencies, among the working class students (Reay, 2002).

So we have attempted to look at and make sense of patterns and effects of choice making in a variety of ways through our questionnaire data, and focus group, observation and interview materials. We are attempting something akin to what Nash (1999, p123) calls a 'numbers and narratives methodology', but with an emphasis, in contrast to Nash, on the latter. This involves attending to both 'the constraining and enabling aspects of the economic, cultural and political structures that affects families, schools and students and the complex and creative set of responses' (p123) that these structures call forth when young people 'make decisions about how to utilise [the exchange value of their educational qualifications] after the completion of schooling' (p123).

In the next chapter we outline the theoretical concepts we are using to make sense of our data. Bourdieu's concepts of habitus, capital and field are described and explained before we begin to indicate how habitus as 'the practical mastery people possess of their situations' (Robbins, 1991 p1), and cultural capital as 'subtle modalities in the relationship to culture and language' (Bourdieu, 1977, p82) are at work in the decisions higher education applicants make.

Notes

1 Although it is around this time that redefinitions of what counts as higher education begin to come into play.

2 There are issues we do not have the space to explore here about what class constitutes. Clearly, acquiring a degree results in a very different experience of being working class for the parents with degrees to those without them. But it is important also to recognise that there is no unitary experience of gaining a degree. For example the uncredentialled mother or father who goes to night school to acquire a degree has a very different experience to the eighteen year old who goes straight from school to university with 3 A levels.

2

Conceptualising choice of higher education

igher education choice takes place within two registers of meaning and action. One is cognitive/performative and relates to the matching of performance to the selectivity of institutions and courses. The other is social/cultural and relates to social classifications of self and institutions. What we are trying to do in this chapter is to understand how higher education choice is exercised in different ways for different groups of students across both registers and have found Bourdieu's theoretical framework useful. The first part of this chapter outlines the concepts we have drawn on, while in the second part we begin to examine higher education choice through the lens of Bourdieu's conceptual framework. Using case studies, we illustrate how habitus and cultural capital provide a way of understanding the decisions higher education applicants make.

Section 1 Conceptual starting points
Cultural capital

Bourdieu sees his concept of cultural capital as breaking with the received wisdom that attributes academic success or failure to natural aptitudes, such as intelligence and giftedness. In contrast, Bourdieu explains school success by the amount and type of cultural capital inherited from the family milieu rather than by measures of individual talent or achievement:

> The notion of cultural capital initially presented itself to me, in the course of research, as a theoretical hypothesis which made it possible to explain the unequal scholastic achievement of children originating from different social classes by relating academic success, i.e., the specific profits which children from the different classes and class fractions can obtain in the academic market, to the distribution of cultural capital between the classes and class fractions. (Bourdieu, 1986, p243)

For Bourdieu cultural capital encompasses a broad array of linguistic competences, manners, preferences and orientations, which, Bourdieu terms 'subtle modalities in the relationship to culture and language' (Bourdieu, 1977, p82). Bourdieu identifies three variants of cultural capital. The first is in the embodied state incorporated in mind and body. The accumulation of cultural capital in its embodied form begins in early childhood. It requires pedagogical action, the investment of time by parents, other family members or hired professionals to sensitise the child to cultural distinctions. We glimpse the workings of this form of cultural capital later in the chapter, and throughout the book, particularly in the narratives of young people from established middle class families. Second, cultural capital exists in the institutionalised state, that is in institutionalised forms such as educational qualifications, and third, in the objectified state, simply existing as cultural goods such as books, artefacts, dictionaries and paintings (Bourdieu, 1984). We can see here that cultural capital is much more than the high status activities that have traditionally been operationalised in empirical research within education (Ganzeboom *et al*, 1990; Kastillis and Rubinson, 1990; Mohr and DiMaggio, 1995; Aschaffen and Maas, 1996; Sullivan, 2001; Dumais, 2002).

In this book we are working with a broad understanding of cultural capital, one that focuses on qualitative dimensions of cultural capital as well as the measurable, and emphasises 'the affective aspects of inequality' (Skeggs, 1997, p10), such as levels of confidence, certainty, and entitlement. Whilst recognising more straightforward aspects of cultural capital like educational qualifications and participation in high status activities, we would stress the importance of these more subjective aspects. It is these aspects of cultural capital, often underplayed in other empirical studies utilising

Bourdieu's concepts, that are key dimensions of cultural capital across social fields. In their critical assessment of cultural capital in educational research Annette Lareau and Elliot Weininger (2003, p2) argue for a conceptualisation that focuses on 'micro-interactional processes whereby individuals' strategic use of knowledge, skills and competence comes into contact with institutionalised standards of evaluation'. Throughout this book we illustrate through students' and their parents' narratives, the myriad ways in which an individual's ability to deploy knowledge, skills and competences successfully is powerfully classed. In particular, we illustrate the salience of confidence, certainty and sense of entitlement that is generated through high levels of cultural capital relevant to those struggles for position which take place in the field of education.

Cultural capital is not the only capital accruing to individuals. It is primarily a relational concept and exists in conjunction with other forms of capital. Therefore, it cannot be understood in isolation either from the habitus that generates it or the other forms of capital that, alongside cultural capital, constitute advantage and disadvantage in society. These include economic, symbolic and social capital. Social capital is generated through social processes between the family and wider society and is made up of social networks. Economic capital is wealth, either inherited or generated from interactions between the individual and the economy, while symbolic capital is manifested in individual prestige and personal qualities, such as authority and charisma (Bourdieu, 1985b). In addition to their interconnection, Bourdieu envisages a process in which one form of capital can be transformed into another. For example, economic capital can be converted into cultural capital by buying an elite education, while cultural capital can be readily translated into social capital.

The overall capital of different fractions of the social classes is composed of differing forms and volumes of the various kinds of capital (Bourdieu, 1993). It is mainly in relation to the middle and upper classes that Bourdieu elaborates this variation in volume and composition of the four types of capital. For example, individuals can be adjacent to each other in social space yet have very different ratios of economic to cultural capital. These differences are a consequence of complex relationships between individual and class trajectories. Moreover, the value attached to the different forms of capital are stakes in the struggle between different class fractions. Bourdieu uses the analogy of a game of roulette to describe how some individuals might play:

> those with lots of red tokens and a few yellow tokens, that is lots of economic capital and a little cultural capital will not play in the same way as those who have many yellow tokens and a few red ones .....the more yellow tokens (cultural capital) they have, the more they will stake on the yellow squares (the educational system). (Bourdieu, 1993, p34)

Habitus

Habitus, in contrast, is less well known and is probably Bourdieu's most contested concept. Unlike cultural capital, habitus has been subject to widespread criticism, mainly on the basis of its latent determinism and inaccessibility to empirical study. This is ironic in view of Bourdieu's rationale for developing the concept. He argues that habitus is central to his methodology of structuralist constructivism, an attempt to transcend dualisms of agency-structure, and objective-subjective. Habitus then is the conceptual tool that Bourdieu uses in an attempt to reconcile these dualisms (Bourdieu, 1985a). According to Bourdieu it is through the workings of habitus that practice (agency) is linked with capital and field (structure). In relation to the charge of determinism Bourdieu (1990b, p116) argues that habitus becomes active in relation to a field, and the same habitus can lead to very different practices and stances depending on the state of the field. One way of unpacking just what Bourdieu meant by habitus is to analyse it in terms of four related aspects (Reay, 2004).

The first key aspect of habitus is that it is embodied. Instead of working with what he considers to be a flawed conceptualisation, that of the 'active subject confronting society as if that society were an object constituted externally' (Bourdieu, 1990b, p190), Bourdieu developed the concept of habitus to demonstrate not only the ways in which the body is in the social world, but also the ways in which the social world is in the body (Bourdieu, 1981). The habitus:

> Is a socialised body. A structured body, a body which has incor-
> porated the immanent structures of a world or of a particular
> sector of that world – a field – and which structures the perception
> of that world as well as action in that world. (Bourdieu, 1998a, p81)

Thus, one of the crucial features of habitus is that it is embodied;
it is not composed solely of mental attitudes and perceptions (Shilling, 2004). Bourdieu writes that it is expressed through durable
ways 'of standing, speaking, walking, and thereby of feeling and
thinking' (Bourdieu, 1990a, p70). People's relationships to dominant culture are conveyed in a range of activities, including eating,
speaking and gesturing (Bourdieu, 1984). So the habitus as the
social is inscribed in the body of the biological individual (Bourdieu,
1985b, p113).

The second key aspect of habitus is its ability to hold both structure
and agency in tension. Far from viewing habitus as a latent tendency, Bourdieu sees habitus as potentially generating a wide
repertoire of possible actions, simultaneously enabling the individual to draw on transformative and constraining courses of action.
He writes that:

> Habitus is a kind of transforming machine that leads us to 'repro-
> duce' the social conditions of our own production, but in a
> relatively unpredictable way, in such a way that one cannot move
> simply and mechanically from knowledge of the conditions of pro-
> duction to knowledge of the products. (1993, p87)

However, as the quote reveals, the addendum in Bourdieu's work
is always an emphasis on the constraints and demands which impose themselves on people. While the habitus allows for individual
agency it also predisposes individuals towards certain ways of
behaving:

> The habitus, as a system of dispositions to a certain practice, is an
> objective basis for regular modes of behaviour, and thus for the
> regularity of modes of practice, and if practices can be predicted
> ...this is because the effect of the habitus is that agents who are
> equipped with it will behave in a certain way in certain circum-
> stances. (Bourdieu, 1990b, p77)

Yet despite this implicit tendency to behave in ways that are expected of people like us, for Bourdieu there are no explicit rules or
principles which dictate behaviour, rather 'the habitus goes hand in

hand with vagueness and indeterminacy' (Bourdieu, 1990b, p77). The practical logic which defines habitus is not one of the predictable regularity of modes of behaviour, but instead 'that of vagueness, of the more-or-less, which defines one's ordinary relation to the world' (Bourdieu, 1990b, p78). However, at other times, Bourdieu does point out that the operation of the habitus regularly excludes certain practices: those which are unfamiliar to the cultural groupings to which the individual belongs. We can see examples of this throughout the book with young privileged middle class applicants talking in terms of always taking it for granted that they would go to university, while their working class counterparts felt, for the most part, that the more elite universities were not for the likes of them. In chapter five we discuss such working class examples of 'making a virtue out of necessity' (Bourdieu, 1990a, p54). Working class acquiescence, a propensity to accept exclusion or exclude oneself rather than attempt to achieve what is already denied, arises because the dispositions, which make up habitus, are the products of opportunities and constraints framing the individual's earlier life experiences. According to Bourdieu they are:

> durably inculcated by the possibilities and impossibilities, freedoms and necessities, opportunities and prohibitions inscribed in the objective conditions. (Bourdieu, 1990a, p54)

As a result, improbable practices are rejected as unthinkable and only a limited range of practices is possible.

Habitus can also be understood as a compilation of collective and individual trajectories. Bourdieu conceives of habitus as a multilayered concept, with more general notions of habitus at the level of society and more complex, differentiated notions at the level of the individual. A person's individual history is constitutive of habitus but so also is the whole collective history of family and class that the individual is a member of. Thus for Bourdieu 'the subject is not the instantaneous ego of a sort of singular cogito, but the individual trace of an entire collective history' (Bourdieu, 1990b, p91).

At times Bourdieu seems to be suggesting a degree of uniformity. At other times, he recognises differences and diversity between members of the same cultural grouping and writes in terms of the singularity of individual habitus. Habitus within, as well as between, social groups differs to the extent that the details of individuals' social trajectories diverge from one another: 'Just as no two individual histories are identical so no two individual habituses are identical' (Bourdieu, 1993, p46).

However, because there are classes of experience there are also classes of habitus or the habitus of classes. Bourdieu attempts to justify his collective definition of habitus. In reference to class habitus he asserts that:

> interpersonal relations are never, except in appearance, individual-to-individual relationships and that the truth of the interaction is never entirely contained in the interaction. (Bourdieu, 1990b, p81)

A collective understanding of habitus is necessary, according to Bourdieu, in order to recognise that individuals contain within themselves their past and present position in the social structure 'at all times and in all places, in the forms of dispositions which are so many marks of social position' (Bourdieu, 1990b, p82).

Habitus' duality as both collective and individualised offers theoretical potential, but also, as Cicourel (1993) points out, conceptual difficulties. Bourdieu often refers to class habitus and a number of researchers have also worked with the concept of class habitus (Bourdieu and Passeron, 1979; Bridge, 2001; Hartmann, 2002; James, 1995; Sawchuk, 2003). The largest and most comprehensive research study of class habitus is Bourdieu's own study of Distinction in French society (1984). Although the study draws on both quantitative and qualitative data, because habitus cannot be directly observed in empirical research and has to be apprehended interpretively, much of Distinction is devoted to a qualitative study of the myriad artistic/culinary preferences and practices which cluster in each sector of social space, that is within each class and class fraction, in order to identify the specific habitus that underlies them (Weininger, 2004). There is also a further strand of research that works with institutional notions of habitus (Barber, 2002; McDonough, 1997, McNamara Horvat and Lising Antonio, 1999; Reay, 1998; Reay et al, 2001), and this has proved a particularly productive way of making sense of the differences between the six very different educational institutions in the study (see chapter 3).

It is also helpful to see habitus as a complex interplay between past and present. Bourdieu actually writes that habitus 'refers to something historical, it is linked to individual history' (1993, p86). Individual histories therefore are vital to understanding the concept of habitus. Habituses are permeable and responsive to what is going on around them. Current circumstances are not just there to be acted upon, but are internalised and become yet another layer to add to those from earlier socialisations:

> The habitus acquired in the family is at the basis of the structuring of school experiences... the habitus transformed by the action of the school, itself diversified, is in turn at the basis of all subsequent experiences ...and so on, from restructuring to restructuring. (Bourdieu, 1972, cited in Bourdieu and Wacquant, 1992, p134)

Therefore, although the habitus is a product of early childhood experience, and in particular socialisation within the family, it is continually modified by individuals' encounters with the outside world (Di Maggio, 1979). Schooling, especially, acts to provide a general disposition, a turn towards what Bourdieu terms 'a cultured habitus' (Bourdieu, 1967, p344). We have tried to grasp this sense of a general disposition through our analysis of institutional habituses in chapter 3. Dispositions are inevitably reflective of the schooling context in which they are, in part, acquired. For Bourdieu, although habitus reflects the social position in which it was constructed, it also carries within it the genesis of new creative responses, which are capable of transcending the social conditions in which it was produced. Otherwise, we would not have working class applicants. In some ways the working class applicants to university in our study epitomise habitus at its most agentic. Bourdieu writes that habitus is 'the product of social conditionings, and thus of a history' (Bourdieu, 1990b, p116).

Perhaps the range of possibilities inscribed in a habitus are best envisaged as a continuum. At one end habitus can be replicated through encountering a field that reproduces its dispositions. At the other end of the continuum, habitus can be transformed through a process that either raises or lowers an individual's expectations. Implicit in the concept is the possibility of a social trajectory which enables conditions of living that are very different from initial ones.

By drawing together these four themes running through Bourdieu's discussions of habitus, habitus can be viewed as a complex internalised core from which everyday experiences emanate. Choice is at the heart of habitus, which he likens to 'the art of inventing' (Bourdieu, 1990a, p55), but at the same time the choices inscribed in the habitus are limited. Choices are bounded by the framework of opportunities and constraints the person finds herself in, her external circumstances. However, within Bourdieu's theoretical framework she is also circumscribed by an internalised framework which makes some possibilities inconceivable, others improbable and a limited range acceptable.

Working with Bourdieu's concept of habitus and his notion of choice provides us with a very different way of understanding educational choices from those implicit in rational action theory (Breen and Goldthorpe, 1997). Unlike rational action theory which underplays cultural context, the concept of habitus emphasises the enduring influence of a range of contexts, familial, peer group, institutional and class culture, and their subtle, often indirect, but still pervasive influence on choices. It foregrounds the power of implicit and tacit expectations, affective responses and aspects of cultural capital such as confidence and entitlement, often marginalised in academic research. We hope to show throughout the rest of the book both the tensions and the reinforcements between external and internal, structure and agency, that are generated through choices of higher education.

Field

Field can be understood as a particular social setting where class dynamics take place, for example, a classroom or a workplace, but it can also refer to more abstract and broader concerns like the field of politics or the legal field (Silva, 2004). The concept of field adds to the possibilities of Bourdieu's conceptual framework and gives habitus a dynamic quality:

> The relation between habitus and field operates in two ways. On one side, it is a relation of conditioning: the field structures the habitus, which is the product of the embodiment of the immanent necessity of the field (or of a hierarchy of intersecting fields). On the other side, it is a relation of knowledge or cognitive construc-

tion: habitus contributes to constituting the field as a meaningful world, a world endowed with sense or with value, in which it is worth investing one's energy. (Bourdieu in Wacquant, 1989, p44)

Grenfell and James (1998, p15) argue that 'if habitus brings into focus the subjective end of the equation, field focuses on the objective'. It is the interaction of habitus, capital and field that generates the logic of practice. 'The logic of practice lies in being logical to the point at which being logical would cease being practical' (Bourdieu, 1990b, p79).

As Grenfell (2003) succinctly asserts, habitus and field need to be understood as highly charged matrices involving a dynamic philosophy of human praxis. This can produce a powerful synergy in which:

> social reality exists, so to speak, twice, in things and in minds, in fields and in habitus, outside and inside social agents. And when habitus encounters a social world of which it is the product, it is like a 'fish in water': it does not feel the weight of the water and it takes the world about itself for granted. (Bourdieu and Wacquant, 1992, p127)

When habitus encounters a field with which it is not familiar however, the resulting disjunctures can generate change and transformation but also disquiet, ambivalence, insecurity and uncertainty. Implicit in the concept is that habitus operates at an unconscious level unless individuals confront events which cause self-questioning, whereupon habitus begins to operate at the level of consciousness and the person develops new facets of the self. Such disjunctures between habitus and field occur for Bourdieu when individuals with a well-developed habitus find themselves in different fields or different parts of the same social field or when there are social changes affecting a social field. In the chapters that follow we see many 'fish in water' but we also describe processes of disjuncture, particularly when our working class students encounter the elite universities.

Section 2: Putting Bourdieu to work

In this second section of the chapter we draw on the concepts outlined in the first part to show how the perceptions, distinctions and choices of higher education institutions used and made by students play a part in reconstituting and reproducing the divisions and hierarchies in higher education. As Bourdieu (1984) explains:

> The division into classes performed by sociology leads to the common root of the classifiable practices which agents produce and of the classificatory judgements they make of other agents' practices and their own. [...] It is in the relationship between the two capacities which define the habitus, the capacity to produce classifiable practices and works, and the capacity to differentiate and appreciate these practices and products (taste), that the represented social world i.e., the space of lifestyles, is constituted. [...] The habitus is necessity internalised and converted into a disposition that generates meaningful practices and meaning-giving perceptions. (p169-170)

It is in the empirical examination of the relationships between classifiable practices and classificatory judgements in particular fields that habitus – as a generative formula – fleetingly comes into view. Choice of higher education is one such field and moment. What we are suggesting then is that in important respects choice of university is a choice of lifestyle and a matter of taste, and further, that social class is a key aspect of these subtexts of choice. In other words this is choice as class-matching and thus also a form of social closure (Parkin, 1974; Ball, 2003).

As suggested by various studies of educational expansion, as access becomes democratised internal differentiation and differential rates of completion appear to become more significant in relation to social differentiation (Duru-Bellat, 2000; Shumar, 1997). We argue here that alongside the academic and social selectivity of higher education institutions, the relative status and social exclusivity of Universities and the relationship of this to student choice and choice-making are key factors in generating and reproducing patterns of internal differentiation. That is to say, cultural and social capital, material constraints (see Reay et al, 2002), social perceptions and distinctions, and forms of self-exclusion (Bourdieu, 1990a) are all at work in the process of choice.

One of our main aims is to understand how such decision making is exercised differently and works differently for different groups of higher education applicants. Below we glimpse a range of aspects of difference powerfully underpinned by class and ethnic habitus and greatly differing levels of cultural capital:

... I thought that the most important thing would be how respected the degree would be by the architectural community. So when I asked in my work experience place where would be a respected degree, they said: the one that came up a lot was the architectural school at University College, London. And then I actually went to a few open days and I realised the more important thing was the university itself, if I'd enjoy going there. And settled upon Sheffield, basically because of the facilities, and the atmosphere just seemed right, like I would really enjoy three years there, for the degree. And then maybe somewhere else, wherever. But the most important thing was that I was going to spend the next three years of my life wherever, so I had to know that I would feel comfortable there and enjoy it. (Duncan, white English, middle class student, CB)

Socially, or through my family, I don't know anybody who has completed university, you know, I don't know anybody well, who has completed university. My uncle was the first person in my entire family, like, ever, to go to university and complete it, but he died in 1993, so I don't know, I didn't really have time to talk to him about it, or find out anything or get any encouragement, advice or anything like that from him. So I suppose that's maybe why I didn't know about the reputations of the universities or any sort of things like that. Apart from what I was told by the prospectuses, the brochures, computers, what my teachers told me. I sort of worked it out as I went along really, played it by ear. Maybe if I had known some people that had gone to university it might have made my choices different, or maybe not, I don't really know. (Shaun, white Irish, working class student CCS)

Well, just since I've been born, I suppose it's just been assumed I am going to university, because both my parents went to university, all their brothers and sisters went to university and my sister went to university and so I don't know if I've even stopped to think about it. I've always just thought I am going to go to university, and I don't know, I have kind of grown up with the idea that's what people do, most people do that. I mean, quitting school has never been an option for me. If I really wanted to I think my parents would probably support me, but I've just never even considered it as an option, I have always assumed I have been going to university and the choice has just been which university, rather than will I go at all, I suppose that's just the way my parents are, they just send us to university. (Nick, white, middle class student, MU)

I did read about the African Caribbean societies and the Asian societies and all the different things they do, and I know there are quite a few people, a few black people and Asian people who do go to Sussex and Manchester Met and stuff like that and that was important that they had those sorts of societies there. It means you know you're not going to be the only black person there. So I know the population is predominately white in Sussex, but even then that didn't effect me really, because I thought as long as there are some black people there, and there are some Asian people there, and Chinese people there, whatever, I don't mind because I prefer to be somewhere where there is different cultures. And so I did make sure that there was a mix yes.... (Esther, Black, African middle class student CCS)

... Westminster, I have this friend who works with me, and basically, he has just come from Bangladesh, he wants to do a masters in International Relations, and he heard about Westminster when he was in Bangladesh, so I thought maybe its because the university is good for that subject so then I decided to do it. (Kahlil, working class Bangladeshi student CCS)

I think the decision was more economical than anything else, because ideally I would like to travel outside London and live away from home, probably rent a place, ideally, but looking at the reality of how likely it is, its is very, very, very unlikely. It is more sense to say, you know studying inside London, somewhere that is close by, so I can cycle there or take the train. But not too far out. (Ahmed, working class Bangladeshi student CCS)

Ever since Samantha was old enough to know what a doctor was that's all she's ever wanted to do. She just never really needed advice. I mean, yes, she went along to various careers lectures and spoke to teachers and whatever, but she never really was that interested. She always knew what she wanted to do.

Deciding which university was probably a very unscientific process actually. My father went to Trinity in Cambridge to do law. And he was always very keen to show her Cambridge and show her his old college, which he did, when she was probably only about thirteen. And she fell in love with it. And decided that's where she wanted to go. As time progressed and she learnt about step papers and all the other things that you have to do she decided maybe Trinity might be a bit formidable in terms of getting in, because she hasn't got the hugest amount of confidence actually, and she thought that maybe she should look for a college that wasn't quite so difficult, although frankly I'm sure they are all identical. So she started to look at others, but again, not very scientifically.

> She went up on an open day with her careers teacher. And they
> went for an open day at Clare, I think it was, and while she was
> there she also had a look around at some of the other colleges
> including Trinity Hall, but just a quick look. A friend of mine had a
> daughter, who had just taken a place at Trinity Hall to do natural
> sciences and this friend of mine is very, very good at research all
> this sort of stuff and she'd been into it in huge, huge detail and she
> basically gave me the benefit of all her research and said Trinity
> Hall is a much smaller college and they may not require her step
> and her daughter certainly would benefit from a smaller college
> and thought that maybe Samantha might as well, and why didn't
> we look at Trinity Hall? Which is why we looked at Trinity Hall. And
> she spoke to her teachers about it and they agreed she should try
> for Trinity Hall, I don't think anybody else was trying as well, which
> probably helped, and that's how she ended up at Trinity Hall (white
> middle class mother of Samantha, a HG student)

These quotes only begin to scratch the surface of the complexities
of choice. They simply represent some key criteria, often among
many cited, that underpinned student choice. While it is possible to
see the ways in which context, opportunity and emotion are played
out very differently, these quotes also indicate the interplay of
strategic rational action with non-rational or non-utilitarian goals.
As Hatcher (1998, p16) puts it, 'rational choice ... is a significant
element in many transition decisions, but it is neither a necessary
nor a sufficient one'. Duncan, who elsewhere in his interview
talked about going to university as 'following in the family footsteps', uses a combination of institutional status and social opportunities and milieu to frame his choice – finding somewhere where
he is socially comfortable. There are no clear external constraints
acting upon his choice. Nick provides a classic example of a 'fish in
water'. For him going to university is simply the next stage in a
seamless, taken-for-granted, middle class trajectory. Samantha has
not only always known that she would go to university, she has also
always known what she would study and where. All three have
copious reserves of cultural, social and economic capital – in
Samantha's case, to the extent that she does not even need the
school's advice. We can see the ways in which:

> The embodied cultural capital of the previous generation functions
> as a sort of advance (both a head-start and a credit) which, by pro-
> viding from the outset the example of culture incarnated in

> familiar models, enables the newcomer to start acquiring the basic elements of the legitimate culture, from the beginning, that is, in the most unconscious and impalpable way. (Bourdieu, 1984, p70-71)

Young people like Duncan, Samantha and Nick are living out 'a normal biography' (Du Bois-Reymond, 1998). Normal biographies are linear, anticipated and predictable, unreflexive transitions, often gender and class specific, rooted in well-established life-worlds. They are often driven by an absence of decisions. Middle class young people like Duncan, Samantha and Nick talked of going to University as 'automatic', 'taken for granted', 'always assumed'. The decision to go to university is a non-decision. It is rational and it is not. This is the work of 'class wisdom' (Lauder *et al*, 1999); 'intentionality without intention' (Bourdieu, 1990a, p108). As we argued earlier, these middle class young people move in their world as a fish in water and 'need not engage in rational computation in order to reach the goals that best suit their interests' (Bourdieu, 1990a, p108). Decision making comes into play in relation to which university and often their understanding of the right sort of university for them is ingrained, tacit, taken for granted. The privately educated students do not even need to articulate the divide between old and new universities because going to a new university is just not what someone like them does. All four middle class students across ethnic difference and the state-private school divide demonstrate 'the self-assured relationship to the world' (Bourdieu, 1984, p56) of middle class habitus.

All this contrasts with the doubts, ambivalences and very deliberate decision making of many of the working class and ethnic minority young people in our sample, like Shaun, Ahmed and Kalil, who were the first in their families to contemplate higher education.

For example, there is little that is anticipated and familiar in Ahmed's transition to higher education. He is negotiating an unfamiliar field. He is also directly constrained by financial considerations and other criteria clearly take second place. Shaun, who lived independently and worked long hours part-time, was decisively influenced by setting and formed his view of Universities through his own research. Esther, who is West African and also firmly embedded in familial expectations about university attendance, is specifically concerned about the ethnic mix of institutions under consideration. And Kalil chooses subject and institution very much by chance. His view of institutional status is based upon a single piece of 'hot knowledge' (Ball and Vincent, 1998).

For students like Duncan, Samantha, Nick and Esther, choice is primarily related to factors internal to universities themselves. These are real places that have different qualities and characteristics about which judgments have to be made. Middle class students are making judgements of taste and distinction in their choice making. In their narratives we can identify a different class vantage point; a positioning in the field from which choosing a university is a process of middle class taste (Bourdieu, 1984; Ball *et al*, 2000). For those like Ahmed, Shaun and Kahlil, as Archer and Hutchings (2001) put it, university is viewed from the outside and external/extrinsic concerns predominate in choice-making. They are positioned very differently in the higher education field. Even from these brief examples it is possible to begin to see how, in a straightforward sense, habitus as 'the practical mastery which people possess of their situations' (Robbins, 1991, p1), and cultural capital as 'subtle modalities in the relationship to culture and language' (Bourdieu, 1977, p82) are at work in the 'immanent decisions which people actually make...' (Robbins, 1991, p1); that is, within the logic of their practices.

Concluding comments

In this chapter we have introduced and described Bourdieu's concepts of habitus, cultural capital and field. These are the main conceptual tools we have utilised in making sense of our data. In the second part of the chapter we began to examine higher education choice through the lens of Bourdieu's theoretical framework, illustrating how habitus and cultural capital provide a way of understanding the decisions higher education applicants make. In the next chapter we focus on the concept of institutional habitus in order to explore the impact made by individual institutions on the attainment of prospective university applicants and their subsequent destinations within higher education.

3

Making a difference:
institutional habituses

This chapter examines the role of individual institutions, the schools and colleges in our study, and their impact on students and their higher education destinations. Our interview and observational data suggest that 'a school effect' (Smith and Tomlinson, 1989) – what we term institutional habitus – is an intervening variable, providing a semi-autonomous means by which class, raced and gendered processes are played out in the lives of students and their higher education choices.

In the US, Boyle's (1966) study suggested that college aspirations are influenced by the practices of high schools and, in particular the imposition of academic standards. Alwin and Otto's (1977) research mapped the impact of high schools' average ability and SES levels on individuals' ability and SES levels and concomitantly their choices of higher education. Falsey and Heigns (1984) found that privately educated students were significantly more likely than their public school counterparts to go on to prestigious four year higher education institutions even when ability levels, aspirations and social class were controlled for. More recent research in the US (McDonough, 1997) argues that the interplay of a student's social class background and secondary schools' organisational contexts and processes are central to the question of where an individual attends university. In the UK, despite a recent emphasis on the contribution of individual schools and colleges to the qualifications and destinations of young people at the age of sixteen (Cheng, 1995; Smith and Tomlinson, 1989; Ball *et al*, 2000), few studies have focused on the relationships between type of school attended and higher education choice and access.

In this study we have deployed the concept of institutional habitus in order to explore such relationships. As we saw in chapter 2, habitus is a dynamic concept, a rich interlacing of past and present, individual and collective. Bourdieu describes habitus as 'a power of adaptation. It constantly performs an adaptation to the outside world which only occasionally takes the form of radical conversion' (Bourdieu, 1993, p88). Dispositions inevitably reflect the social context in which they are acquired. Any conception of institutional habitus would similarly constitute a complex amalgam of agency and structure and could be understood as the impact of a cultural group or social class on an individual's behaviour as it is mediated through an organisation (McDonough, 1997). Institutional habituses, no less than individual habituses, have a history and have in most cases been established over time. They are therefore capable of change but by dint of their collective nature are less fluid than individual habitus. In earlier work Reay argued that schools and colleges had identifiable institutional habituses and utilised the concept to demonstrate how the organisational cultures of schools and colleges are linked to wider socio-economic cultures through processes in which schools and their catchments mutually shape and reshape each other (Reay, 1998a; Reay *et al*, 2001).

In chapter 4 we explore parental involvement in higher education choice making, drawing on the concept of familial habitus. However, perceptions and expectations of choice are constructed over time in relation to school friends and teachers' views and advice, and learning experiences, no less than in relationship to the views and expectations of families. Whilst recognising how enmeshed familial and institutional habituses are, we demonstrate the significance of an institutional influence over and above the direct impact of family background, although it is clear that some families chose schools for their children to ensure access to particular institutional habituses. This becomes an aspect of the process of forming the child and a guarantee of opportunity and advantage. In such circumstances parents can rest assured that, unless crises occur, they can leave the school to do its work.

In their research on elementary schools in the Netherlands, Rupp and De Lange (1989) develop the concept of educational status which is determined by the level of secondary schooling for which the elementary school prepares its students. Implicit in the concept is the dynamic relationship between the characteristics of a school's intake and its educational status. Applying this concept of educational status to the six institutions in our study we can see that the educational status of a sixth form or FE college (the spectrum of the university hierarchy for which the institution prepares its students) constitutes an important part of institutional habitus. At the same time there are other inter-related elements, most notably curriculum offer, organisational practices and less tangible but equally important cultural and expressive characteristics. These latter aspects, the 'expressive order' of the school, include expectations, conduct, character and manners (Bernstein, 1975). They constitute embodied cultural capital – embodied in the collectivity of students, in their dress, demeanour and stances. They are also often embodied in buildings, trophies, rituals, performances and in the school staff (their histories and qualifications).

Although Martin Thrupp does not use the concept of institutional habitus, his work on school mix illuminates the workings of different aspects of institutional habitus by demonstrating how the numerous differences between schools in group, instructional, organisational and management processes are linked to school composition (Thrupp, 1999). Working with concepts of critical mass and middle class/organic, working class/inorganic relations between home and school, he illustrates the ways in which power relations between different social classes within schools are of central importance. For Thrupp, class-based organic and inorganic relationships are played out at the school level:

> Schools develop processes that reflect their SES mix. Solidly middle class schools have strongly supportive student cultures which allow them to teach an academic, school-based curriculum and to organise and manage themselves relatively smoothly.

Working class students who attend a working class school may often fail not only because of their own background but also because they are attending working class schools which cannot offer middle class types of school resources and processes. Conversely working class students who attend a middle class school are more likely to succeed because they are exposed, despite their individual class backgrounds, to the contextual benefits of a middle class school mix. (Thrupp, 1999, p125-6)

Here we can see how wider socio-economic cultures impact on organisational practices within schools and colleges in ways which, we argue later, also shape opportunities and constraints within the higher education choice process.

Although the main foci for this chapter are the institutional contexts within which students make choices of higher education and the organisational practices that support their decision making, we recognise that the various influences impacting on students' choices cannot be separated out and compartmentalised. Rather, higher education applicants are located within a matrix of influences which are best represented by overlapping circles of individual, family, friends and institution. The relative weight of these spheres of influence are not only different for different individuals but shift and change over time for each student. Yet in spite of an inevitable degree of overlap and blurring of boundaries between peer group, family and institution, we argue that there are specific effects from attending a particular educational institution which become most evident when you look at the choices of similar kinds of students across the private-state divide.

Importantly, individuals are differentially positioned in relation to the institutional habitus of their school or college according to the extent to which influences of family and peer group are congruent or discordant with those of the institution. It is only the more privileged of the middle class students, primarily in the private sector, who experience the different contexts impinging on choice as almost seamless. While this advantaged minority are operating within spheres where the diverse influences are predominantly reinforcing rather than in competition or tension with each other, for the majority of students there is less of a fit between educational institution and family and friends. Most are managing a degree of dissonance, and a significant minority are having to cope with tensions that make choice conflictual and problematic. Whilst recognising this inevitable messiness and complexity of choice, in this chapter we deliberately foreground the impact of the institution attended. We draw on interview, questionnaire and observational data to look at some of the ways in which the various components of institutional habitus – educational status, organisational practices and expressive order – influence the choice-making process and, concomitantly, choices of higher education.

'Careers advice, what careers advice?' Levels of practical support and advice within different institutions

One key aspect of institutional habitus that impacts directly on students' higher education destinations is the quality and quantity of careers advice provided. We examine sources of advice and information available to students in more depth in chapter 7. Here we consider how different institutional habituses transform into widely differing advice practices within institutions. It also becomes evident that there are enormous differences between the state and private sectors in the resourcing of advice about careers and higher education. The jibe 'careers advice, what careers advice?' was made by one of the MU students but at both MU and RC the prevalent student view was that careers advice was largely uninfluential or, at times, actively unhelpful. Students most commonly commented that advice had simply reiterated what they already knew or else had been so inconsequential that they had difficulty recalling what advice had actually been given. The situation in the two private schools was different. Below we describe careers advice at CB but the support was similarly intensive and extensive at HG:

> There is a deputy head of careers as well as myself and then there are about three or four other people that help me quite a lot with various careers matters. We have got a careers consultant that comes in from Apex Careers, he comes in usually two days a week. (Dr Anderson, Head of Careers, CB)

As Dr Anderson indicates, careers advice at CB is a major enterprise. Careers education and guidance is provided by two full-time members of staff, the Head and deputy head of careers, by consultants from Apex Careers, but also by other outside agencies, as well as tutors and subject specialists within the school. The school provided frequent input on careers and subject choice from year 9 onwards, including informal lunchtime seminars when leading professionals in their fields, such as academics, lawyers, journalists and politicians, came to talk to students about their work. These perks were in addition to regular, timetabled input on higher education choice. As Marcus claims, 'by the fourth year they're really making you think along the lines of university, not letting you just get by and make decisions on your own'. It is important to reiterate that institutions in the state sector uniformly had far lower levels of resourcing. They were also often responding to quite different and far more diverse student needs.

So at both FFCS and CCS advice and support is rooted in a recognition of the considerable financial and geographical constraints many of the students are operating under. CCS is located in an inner city area which has many features of inner city deprivation. Two thirds of the students are eligible for free school meals, approximately 75 are in temporary accommodation and a sixth are refugees from a total of nineteen countries. Over a sixth are on the register of special needs. Sue Adams, head of the sixth form at CCS, maps out a very different academic landscape to that of CB. In CCS 45 per cent of the sixth form are studying ordinary level GNVQs and for girls, in particular, 'parents just assume that their education terminates when they finish their GCSEs even though many students do very well in their exams' (Sue Adams, Head of Sixth Form, CCS). She highlights a dissonance between home and school: 'we try and persuade them to stay on. But their parents don't want them to continue'.

In contrast to the push from year 9 in CB to consider both post-16 and post-18 options, staff at CCS have just instituted a year 11 conference where students 'are taken out of lessons for a day and given advice and counselling about options post-sixteen and beyond'. Sue talked repeatedly in her interview about the need to persuade parents to let their children stay on. Unlike the parents at CB and HG who are pushing in the same direction as the school and its staff, at CCS staff and parents are often pulling in opposite directions:

> There is a lot of work that still needs doing because we are still losing students. It's about working at all levels, using home link people, getting parents or their children already at university to come back and using them as positive role models to try and persuade, but ultimately it's a long process because they will have come from communities where none of them have experienced this. So naturally they are suspicious. (Sue Adams, Head of Sixth Form, CCS)

While there is a high degree of congruence between familial and institutional habitus in both HG and CB, CCS is having to deal with a number of tensions embedded in the habitus of the school.

On one level such tensions are inevitable in predominantly working class schools; an attribute of 'inorganic' relations between home and school (Thrupp, 1999; Lareau, 1989; 2004). Yet, tensions of class difference are compounded by ethnicity. Imbrications of gender, ethnicity and class meant that often for the Bangladeshi female students and, to a lesser extent, their brothers, higher education was considered a luxury ill-afforded (see also Connor *et al*, 2004). These tensions are exacerbated by the current funding regimes for schools in which money is tied to individual students. For schools like CCS, under-funded and under pressure, it becomes imperative to ensure as many students stay on post-16 as possible. Yet at the same time there is a recognition that the transition to higher education is extremely difficult for many of the students:

> There is a lot of concern about whether I can possibly afford to do this, whether I can possibly afford to take this risk, to take out student loans and to self finance my education. There's a process of having to sort of say although it is all pretty bleak there is a light at the end of the tunnel. But already some students are worrying, have a lot of anxiety about how will their families afford this. (Sue Adams, Head of Sixth Form, CCS)

Institutional habitus interacts with familial habitus to generate processes in CCS that are quite different to those enacted in the private schools.

One clear consequence is the different focus of teachers' time and energy. Unlike CB and HG, where moving into the sixth form was an automatic process which did not require teacher encouragement, Sue spent a large part of the summer term trying to persuade year 11 students and their parents that staying on into the sixth form would be beneficial. She also regularly spent substantial periods of time at the beginning of the academic year talking to parents of year 13 students about the importance of further qualifications for their children. While many of the CCS students were dealing with a dissonance between familial and institutional habitus which often culminated in a sense that higher education and even sixth form attendance was 'not for the likes of us' (Bourdieu, 1990a), the situation at CB and HG was very different.

In the vast majority of cases at the two private schools, familial habitus 'encounters a social world of which it is the product, it is like a 'fish in water': it does not feel the weight of the water and it takes the world about itself for granted' (Bourdieu and Wacquant, 1992, p127). This taken-for-granted disposition which develops when familial and institutional habituses are in symmetry is evident in Hinal's reasoning. He explains why not going to university was inconceivable, going on to elaborate a considered process of choosing higher education which implicates both institutional and familial habitus:

> Well, for me, it was (inconceivable), because basically people tell me this, that, that, that, regardless of who they are. For example, for universities, people will tell you this is good that is bad, and they did a similar type of thing. People were telling me do these A levels, do those A levels, but ultimately what I did was literally, just stood in the middle and just thought every decision out and crossed them out as I went along. (Hinal, Indian middle class student CB)

Although he does not distinguish between people within the family and school, he clearly locates motivation and information with others in a way that suggests that institutional and familial habitus are working in the same direction and that both are crucial in his decision making.

The contrast between Hinal and Shamina and Ruma's descriptions of the choice process highlights the contrast in the institutional habituses of the two schools:

> I just picked up the ones, it was sort of, I was in a rush and I was panicking because I left it so late, which ones to choose, which

ones to go to, and I just put down, Mr Russell said it would be better to choose these universities, so I just looked it up and said OK then, I'll just choose this. Because I was panicking at the last minute and the deadline was coming. (Shamina, working class Bangladeshi student, CCS)

and:

I started filling my UCAS form at the last minute and I was sort of in a panicking state. I just had to chose six quickly so it was just the ones I knew about. I did it really quickly. I had to... if I could do it again I would take longer and look through things more. It was too much of a panic. (Ruma, working class, Bangladeshi student, CCS)

While Hinal's 'as I went along' implies an unrushed, almost leisurely process, Shamina, Ruma and their friends in CCS talk in terms of 'panic' 'haste' and 'rush'.

Educational status and institutional habitus: limiting the field of possibilities

Our quantitative data reveals the ways in which the 'practical principles of division' (Bourdieu, 1984, p471) and in particular 'the distances that need to be kept' (p472) begin to take on a structural

Table 3: First choice of University by type of school: per cent choosing*

	HGS%	LB%	RTC%	CCS%	MU%	FFEC%	Total
Oxbridge	41	48	5	2	11	0	20
Other 'old' pre-1992	48	44	31	20	41	48	40
'New' post-1992	2	1	32	24	15	44	16
Colleges of HE	4	1	9	10	8		6
Not named	5	6	23	44	25	7	18

* This table records the 'first choice' institutions indicated by students who completed the questionnaire and had made up their mind, as well as those who did not name a first choice.

significance. We can glimpse in the preferred choices of our applicants class habitus or more precisely the habitus of particular class fractions (Ball, 2003; Power *et al*, 2003). Perception, expectation and choice all relate to and play their part in reproducing social structures. The private school students express high levels of preference for Oxbridge and virtually no interest in the post-1992 universities. The FE students do not even consider Oxbridge. It is not 'for the likes of them'. At CCS a significant minority of the predominantly working class ethnic minority students are still uncertain about the unfamiliar field they are trying to negotiate. This distribution of classes and class fractions across, and within, institutions of higher education can be viewed as part of the 'self-production of class collectivities through struggles which simultaneously involve relationships between and within classes and determine the actual demarcation of their frontiers' (Wacquant, 1991, p52). The choices indicated here reinforce the divisions and distinctions between higher education institutions noted in chapter 1 and the relationship between social and institutional habituses.

Curriculum offer is an integral part of institutional habitus and underpins the educational status of institutions. Subject preferences highlight curricula differences between the state and the private sectors, with traditional academic subjects predominant in the private sector schools and new subjects more in evidence in the four state sector institutions.

Options at both GCSE and A level in the private schools anticipate choice of traditional subjects at traditional universities. In table 4 we can see that both single subject sciences, medicine and the humanities are popular. In contrast, the state sector has high numbers of media studies, social sciences, business studies choices and other new and vocational subjects. There is a greater match with similar new subjects at new and redbrick universities. Such choices are not simply classed, they are also complexly gendered and racialised within the institutions as certain sorts of courses are talked up by tutors and teachers. Business and accountancy is particularly popular in the tertiary college among ethnic minority students and Art most popular with the MU girls.

Table 4 Choice of university subject by school*

	CB	HG	RC	CCS	MU	FFEC
Social science/ economics	2	6	4	3	6	7
Drama/film/ media			8	1	9	
Education/ nursing/ PE/sport		1	3		10	4
Art	1	1	3		15	
History/ humanities/ archaeology	7	6			4	2
Applied sciences/ computing/ earth sciences	10		2	2	4	6 (all computing)
Pure science	3	10	1	2	1	
Accountancy/ business	1	2	21	1	4	
Medicine	10	9	3	1	2	

* This table records the course choices indicated by students who completed the questionnaire and who were sure, at the time, of their preferred course of study at university. We have just included the most popular subjects because they provide the best indication of trends across the six institutions

The six institutions in the study covered a wide range of educational status (Rupp and De Lange, 1989), from HG and CB, both preparing their students for elite universities, to CCS where, as we have already described, the poverty and deprivation of the catchment area means, as one sixth form tutor exclaimed, 'even getting to university is a miracle'. While HG declares in its brochure for parents that the school 'is selective and the atmosphere unashamedly academic', CCS is struggling to retain a viable year 13 in the face of high drop-out rates. Comments made by two students at the schools encapsulate the difference in institutional habituses. For Hugh, a white English middle class student at CB, 'you've got it all laid out on a plate', while Phu Ca, a Chinese working class student at CCS, claims 'we are really really struggling'. In such starkly opposed circumstances of advantage and disadvantage a good choice means different things and translates into very different options. Below we try to develop further what a good choice signifies within differing institutional contexts.

Articulating similar attitudes to those expressed by Roker's privately educated girls (Roker, 1993), George, a white English middle class student at CB explains that it is expected that students would apply for a good university at his private boys' school:

> My application from here is quite typical of everyone applying in that there are the top twenty universities and people do look at them like this, these are the ones CB apply to.

Dr Anderson, the head of careers, makes explicit the link between good and elite for the majority of boys and their parents at CB:

> A good university is a university that has been there for a long time, and is well-established generally... I think there is a sort of status feeling, you know, the highest status is to go to Oxford and Cambridge, the next one is to be going to Durham, Exeter or Bristol, and you go there regardless of how good the course is in your particular subject.

Dr Anderson's comment is one of many in the transcripts that illustrate the extent to which institutional habitus, shaped by or responding to the dominant familial habitus, limits the universe of possible university choices to a smaller range of manageable considerations. Almost all the students make their higher education choices within constraints – but the sorts of constraints vary enormously.

Processes of delimitation are also evident in both the FE college and CCS, but generate different outcomes for the students to those at CB. For example, at the FE college advice and support is shaped by a recognition of not only the necessity to think local but also of existing prejudices, particularly in the elite universities, towards access students. A good choice is one which builds on longstanding relationships with a number of local higher education institutions which have developed mature student friendly admissions policies. The college has strong connections with two such local universities and as Olivia, a lecturer, comments:

> We know from experience that some of the higher education organisations aren't very sympathetic to mature students, and we politely and discreetly suggest to our students that they don't apply there, because we know they will be very unhappy or they will drop out, because we have got them to this stage, we have sweated blood over these students and we don't want them to fail at the next hurdle, so there are some places we know are very sympathetic and very supportive, and ex-students have been very happy there, and those are the places we'll encourage students to apply to.

Making connections within the field of higher education

Both Dr Anderson's and Olivia's remarks highlight the importance of a further field of institutional habituses. Framing the institutional habituses of the schools and colleges are the institutional habituses of the universities. The degree of coupling (Weick, 1976) between schools/colleges and universities is a manifestation of educational status and clearly has a bearing on student choice. The FE college has instituted processes of strong coupling with two universities which are reflected in the percentage of students applying to them; 32 per cent of the humanities access students moving on to university in Autumn 2000 went to Roehampton, while a further 25 per cent were going to SOAS (the School of Oriental and Asian Studies). Less formalised, although also influential, as we have seen, is the guidance about where not to apply, rooted in lecturers' perceptions that many of the traditional universities are unwelcoming places for mature students.

Institutional habitus has a significant impact which permeates the choice making processes in all six institutions, making some choices virtually unthinkable, others possible and yet others routine (Bourdieu, 1984). However, this does not operate uniformly for all students (see also Reay, 1998a). The extent to which institutional habitus could be mobilised differentially for different groups of students was particularly evident in relation to Oxbridge applicants.

Sponsorship by the school is a valuable asset in a period of credential inflation and Oxbridge candidates in both the private and state sectors gain a significantly greater input from their institutions than those who are applying to less elite universities. Being selected as Oxbridge candidates increases the possibility of augmenting profits of academic and cultural capital regardless of a student's institutional base. As Philip Brown points out:

> Credential inflation is intensifying the competition for credentials from elite universities because degree holders stand 'relative' to one another in a hierarchy of academic and social worth. When market crowding occurs, employers become more discerning about the 'status' of credentials. A degree from Oxbridge or an Ivy League university is judged to have greater capital value than one from a little-known university or college in the market for jobs. (Brown, 1996: 741)

The relationship between Oxbridge and private sector schools is a further, well documented coupling (Smithers, 2000). Oxbridge, despite its recently professed interest in taking more state students, is still struggling with decades of in-built bias in favour of the private sector. In both CB and HG informal connections between teachers and Oxbridge colleges are clear. Not only are there more teachers with Oxbridge backgrounds than in the state sector, for example, 24 per cent of the current staff at HG had been to Oxbridge, but there is also a culture of entitlement; an implicit presumption of compatibility in relation to Oxbridge that does not exist to anything like the same extent in the state schools. Gambetta (1987) asserts in relation to school leavers' higher education choices that students jump as far as they are able.

The private schools could offer information about, contacts with, and visits to Oxbridge which made choice of Oxbridge real and realisable. For many private school students such a choice also followed family traditions.

An article in the *Evening Standard*, a London-based newspaper, describes Oxbridge as 'just a short hop and skip' away from HG; a relatively easy jump in Gambetta's terms. Arabella's text underlines this sense of proximity; a generalised feeling in HG that Oxbridge is the most appropriate place to move on to. Indeed her words show how expectations can move beyond a simple obviousness to become a pressure:

> The school has a strong view that I should go to Cambridge, And they've got a sort of general view that that's the best thing to do full stop... so yeah, they think I should go to Cambridge, so that has been a pressure. (Arabella, white English, middle class student, HG)

Her comments are reinforced time and time again by other HG students:

> It's definitely suggested to girls that they apply. Everyone who has got a chance of getting in is encouraged to apply. They're really keen for girls to go to Oxbridge. (Martina, white European, middle class student, HG)

and:

> Teachers were kind of pressuring me to apply to Oxbridge. Then I got grades for my modules last summer, which were really bad, and I decided there was no way I was going to apply to Cambridge, and then because the teachers here were so encouraging in the end I did. (Rebecca, white English, middle class student, HG)

Thirty per cent of HG girls went on to either Oxford or Cambridge in Autumn 2000, while in CB 19 per cent of the boys gained Oxbridge places for the same academic year. CB's school brochure stresses that 'the most prestigious providers of higher education are targeted and typically 40 per cent of year 13 will apply for Oxbridge places'. In contrast, no one applied for Oxbridge in either FFCS or CCS, while in both RC and MU approximately 6 per cent applied and less than 1 per cent of students gained places. In MU, out of a total of 329 year thirteen students for the academic year 2000/2001, there were only twenty applicants and only three gained a place – although 30 of the students went on to achieve three As at A level. Two of these three had moved to MU's sixth form from private schools perhaps carrying the possibility of Oxbridge with them. They then contribute to the percentage of Oxbridge state school entrants. For the most part in this inner city comprehensive, any sense of entitlement or assurance of compatibility is difficult to sustain within an institution where Oxbridge was frequently viewed as 'not for the likes of us' (Bourdieu, 1990a), even by the high achieving students.

The lack of fit between familial and institutional habituses and the elite field of Oxbridge is captured in Mrs Milner's (MU) explanation of why her daughter failed to gain a place at Cambridge despite achieving three As at A level:

> I'm very angry. I'm very angry with the school – basically the support and help about applying to Oxbridge was pathetic. And I'm angry with Cambridge. Although they are supposed to be making allowances for state students they really didn't. They didn't make allowances in the interview. They might have at the selection stage, for the fact that she hadn't had any of the coaching or groundings and she hadn't gone to the summer school because we hadn't thought about Oxbridge at that point. You know, whereas some of her friends who'd come from private school had because their parents were more into it from the start. She just hadn't got the knowledge they expected her to have and they made no allowances, no allowances at all. (Mrs Milner, mother of working class student at MU)

And later in the interview:

> Anne's peer group at MU is against, certainly against Oxford and Cambridge because they have this kind of traditional stereotype of them being for the upper classes, you know, an elite. And that they wouldn't want to mix with those kind of people. And I think most of her friends felt that very strongly. I think very few students from MU apply to Oxbridge and according to Anne they've nearly all come from private schools.

While both MU's lack of know-how and the powerful influence of the student peer group culture come across strongly in Mrs Milner's words, underlying both HG and CB's activities are long standing, familiar, comfortable relationships with a number of Oxbridge colleges, in which key members of staff have close contact with dons at a range of colleges. Academic social capital, which we explore as a family asset in chapter 4, also operates at the institutional level. Both the private schools have the academic social capital necessary to cultivate close, friendly networks with Oxbridge, while state schools like MU and CCS are still desperately trying to establish productive links. These intimate connections are made explicit by an English middle class mother at CB when she explains why her son applied to a particular Oxford college:

> He's applied to St Hughes, because Mr King teaches history and has just been there six months on a sabbatical leave, so we left it

up to the school. We had, at this point, been I suppose encouraging him slightly to apply to Worcester .... And then the school came back and said they had connections with St Hugh's and they advised him to apply there so we said, you know, the school knows what they are talking about.

In contrast, MU's attempts to sponsor potential applicants were being conducted in circumstances of considerably less access to the academic social capital that counted and, despite demonstrating considerable initiative, had a slightly desperate feel of stabbing in the dark. For example, in her letter to an Oxford college, MU's head of sixth form writes in support of two students' applications:

Both students are considered to be exceptional and achieved highly at GCSE, despite considerable social and material disadvantage. Moira has received free school meals throughout her education. She is the daughter of a lone parent who is dependent on Income Support to maintain the family. Debbie is also from a working class background and has shown considerable personal courage in dealing with her medical condition. I understand Cambridge is very keen to increase its comprehensive intake and sincerely hope these factors will be taken into account when Moira and Debbie are interviewed. (letter sent to Oxford by Ms Keen, Head of Sixth Form, MU)

Here there is no cosy intimate connection; none of CB and HG's extensive network of contacts with Oxbridge, and Ms Keen has to rely on a much more distanced, formalised contact couched in the tones of appeal. Despite her advocacy, neither Moira or Debbie are offered a place.

Spatial notions of proximity and distance provide a useful way of understanding the relationships of different educational institutions to the field of higher education. As is evident above, CB and HG are located institutionally in far greater proximity to Oxbridge and other elite universities than any of the four other institutions. FFCS and CCS, in contrast, have similarly close relationships with the new universities but are far more distant from elite universities. For schools like CCS Oxbridge is beyond the horizon. RC and MU are best represented as equidistant between the elite and new universities. They are both institutionally located further away from elite universities than CB and HG on one side and further away from the new universities than FFCS and CCS on the other, whilst occupying a space closer to redbrick universities than any of the other institutions. This spatial representation maps out a geography of taken-for-granteds, possibilities, improbabilities, relationships and identities. Some routes are much more obvious and straight-forward from one institutional vantage point than another. The perceptions and appreciations embedded in this landscape of choices maps out 'one's relationship to the world and one's proper place in it' (Bourdieu, 1984, p474).

The partial and specific nature of students' higher education knowledge

In chapter 7 we discuss students' different levels of market aware-ness in more depth, but here we examine the relationship between students' higher education knowledge and institutional habitus. Lesley Pugsley (1998) argues that higher education applicants in the ten institutions in her research study displayed very different levels of market awareness. In this research there was a similarly wide spectrum of knowledge about the higher education market in which high levels of market awareness were partial and specific. Students needed to be aware of particular segments of the higher education market depending on their own specific positioning within the field, which in turn, as we have seen, is influenced by institutional habitus. This was particularly the case for the FE students, the private school students and those at CCS.

The greater regulatory power of the private institutions means that their processes of guidance and channelling, in combination with a fairly homogeneous class intake, contribute to a higher degree of uniformity and a narrower range of choices among students than is normally the case in the state sector. Rebecca's words encapsulate the academic steering prevalent in the two private schools:

> The school definitely pressured me. I don't know if that's because they want more people to go to Oxbridge, so it'll be in their league table or whatever. There was certainly quite a lot of pressure for me to apply. But I think it was more a kind of personal thing, they thought I'd enjoy it. And the reason that I was wary about it was just because I was scared of getting turned down and they talked me through that. They said I was setting my standards too low. (Rebecca, white Jewish middle class student, HG)

Such pressure, which was mentioned by over half of the HB students interviewed, is partly to do with the kind of student Rebecca represents and her proper place in the hierarchy of higher education. She is middle class and has been predicted three As. Yet similar students at MU who were also predicted 3 As reported no such pressure. The two schools were responding differently to similar kinds of students, which suggests that institutional habitus is having an impact over and above any family background influences. In a sense the school is doing its job. For many parents this kind of preparation and channelling is what they are paying for. Economic capital is converted into cultural, social and symbolic capital.

Awareness of the relative ranking of elite universities was extremely difficult to avoid, given the institutional habituses of CB and HG. Consequently, the vast majority of students had detailed, well-informed knowledge of the 'premier division' while their understanding of the market positioning of new universities was blurred and ill-informed. In the academic year 2000/2001 only 8 per cent of the boys at CB went on to attend new universities, nearly all because they had failed to achieve the grades required by the traditional universities they had initially applied to.

The extent, then, to which institutional habitus sets parameters around the possible varied considerably between different institutions. The two private schools, the FE college and CCS all have institutional habituses which impose narrower boundaries round choice than in either of the two large state sixth forms, MU and RC. CCS is the only one of the three state sixth forms with an institutional habitus that generates as narrow a range of possibilities as the two private schools, but there the similarity ends. Earlier we noted the enormous differences in the intakes to CB and HG on the one hand and CCS on the other. The contrast between CCS and the private schools in terms of destinations is equally stark. In CCS 60 per cent of year 13 went on to attend new universities, 20 per cent went into the labour market, 10 per cent went to do further courses at FE colleges and only 10 per cent took up places at redbrick universities. No one went to Oxbridge or any other of the elite universities.

The institutional habitus of FFCS also set narrow boundaries around choice. Access courses provide a context independent of the family, schooling and social networks which prevented higher study in adolescence (Ganzeboom and Treiman, 1991). This greater degree of separation from other possible influences increases the impact that FE colleges can exert over choices. Paradoxically, the greater freedom and distance from other conventional sources of influence, the mature students' relatively autonomous decision making in relation to both friends and family, apart from the constraints of obligation, means that they, no less than the private students, are subject to a more powerful institutional habitus than would generally be found in the non-selective state sector:

> People are very passionate in places like this, being a woman, being a single mother, being black, being gay. You know, there is no doubt about it, but it is something that is a major issue for these people and they think that these things are going to be held against them when they go to interview and they feel places like UCL, King's and LSE won't want students like them but it just isn't true anymore. (Sophie, white middle class FE student)

As Sophie's comment and the one by Olivia both indicate, institutional habitus has as strong a channeling and guiding influence for many of the mature students as it has for the private school students, but for different reasons. While for the latter institutional and familial habituses are often closely aligned, for the mature students it is usually the case that the influences of family and friends outside the college are relatively weak compared to that of the educational institution. Certainly, most of the mature students reported little advice or influence from their families of origin. In such a situation the impact of the dominant cultural group or social class within the college on individuals' behaviour can become especially powerful.

Collective versus individualised processes

The extent to which decision making is a collectivised or individualised process constitutes part of 'the expressive order of an institution' (Bernstein, 1975), and is a further aspect of the organisational practices, attitudes and assumptions which make up institutional habitus. In our study, there were marked differences between the FE college and other institutions, in particular CB and MU, in the extent to which higher education decision making was a collective rather than an individualised process. The FE students were much more likely to use the collective 'we' when discussing the choice process, while students in the schools invariably used an individualised 'I'. Alison Kirton (1999) refers to the collaborative ethos underpinning the access course she researched. In FFCS the higher education choice process seemed to be underpinned by cooperation particularly in contrast to the private schools, where the process was far more competitive.

The two sets of fieldnotes from interview practice lessons in FFCS and CB underscore this difference. In the FE college the session was set up as a collaborative exercise, with the students organised in groups of four; one interviewee, one interviewer and two observers charged with providing positive feedback. The tutor's instructions to the class were 'to be as supportive and positive as possible'. In CB the session was organised differently. The two boys chosen as interviewee and interviewer were positioned at the front of the class and the rest of the students were instructed to challenge and point out weaknesses, as well as giving the interviewee scores out of ten for both content and performance. FFCS was also the only institution where students were explicitly encouraged to work together on their personal statements.

Both the FE tutors and the FE students also talked extensively about processes of mutual support which were far less evident elsewhere, although there was a slight tendency, which cut across institutional differences, for females to collaborate more than males. For instance, the young women at both CCS and MU seemed to have been sharing advice much more than either the boys at CCS and MU, or students in the other three schools. In particular, three pairs of girls (four working class and two middle class) at MU collaborated over both subject choice and university destination while there were no examples of boys working together in relation to the choice process. As Maguire *et al* (2000) found in relation to post-16 choice, 'young women were better at supporting one another and sharing information'. However, it was only at FFCS that there were sustained collaborative processes:

The other students that I'm working with, as well, they have been very helpful. A few of them, Carly and Debbie looked at it for me, gave me advice sort of thing. (Darren, Black Caribbean working class FE student)

The other students have all been very supportive. Everybody helps each other, you'll say I'm thinking of applying for Middlesex or SOAS and someone has either been there or knows someone studying there so there's lots and lots of sharing of information. I guess I've learnt a hell of a lot from the other students. (Rick, white English working class FE student)

We are all a really great bunch, we get on terribly well, we are very supportive of each other, both academically and personally. And everybody really helps each other out, if someone has got a problem with something, or they have an obstacle block ... it really is a very good support network. (Lesley, White English FE student from intermediate middle class background although self-identified as working class)

In contrast, the school students map out a far more individualised process:

Talking to friends hasn't been helpful. Not at all. Because everyone's in their own little world. Everyone's concerned about what they are going to do. So everyone goes – OK, if that's what you want to do. And they haven't helped, no. (Sheila, Black English working class student, MU)

Quite a lot I did on my own actually, because most people were like panicking for their own sake and too busy to talk to you so... (Shamina, Bangladeshi working class student, SCCS)

Diane: And did you talk much with friends about it?

Susie: Not really. Maybe a bit. It depends on what course people wanted to do and stuff. Mostly where we decided to apply to, but not really. We mostly did it on our own. (Susie, white English middle class, MU)

I don't know why I haven't discussed it with any of my friends here, but I don't think anyone has much. I think it's quite sort of, I think everyone finds it quite a personal thing, what they want to do and where they go. And I don't think my attitude has influenced my friends that much, hardly at all really. (Tom, white, English middle class, MU)

When we compare the FE college with the two private schools, MU and RC, which have predominantly middle class intakes, the more collectivised approach at FFCS and the more individualised approach to decision making in the schools can only be attributed to class differences among the students. However, CCS, with a similar social class profile to FFCS, shared the individualised approach of the more middle class institutions. We would argue that the difference is as much a consequence of institutional as of familial habitus. The expressive order in FFCS, in direct contrast to those of the other five institutions, gives explicit primacy to collegial ways of working and interacting.

But overt processes only tell part of the story of institutional influences. Equally important are the less concrete, more intangible elements. In this regard there were key issues around institutional habituses and indirect collective processes of higher education choice. While the boys at CB and particularly the girls at CCS were not helping each other in the direct ways evident at the FE college, they were having an influence on each other's choices – an influence that came through both institutional ethos and peer pressure, as Omar, a middle class Iranian student, explains in relation to CB:

> If you take a group of ten people and nine people have applied to these sorts of universities, like London ones, or you know, prestigious ones, and you don't really want to feel like – I am going to apply to this place just because I want to. And they will say – why are you doing that? Why don't you join the flow? This tends to happen.

Omar applied to do medicine, which is a popular subject choice at his private boys' school but fails to gain the necessary grades. In a telephone interview after the publication of the A level results he asserts that his poor grades were 'really a blessing in disguise because he can now pursue a career in Art':

> Now I can do design. Hardly anyone applies to Art College here, it's like it's just not the done thing, too low status or something but it really is what I want to do and doing badly's given me the chance so now I'm going to Chelsea Art College and I'm really pleased about it. I think it's going to be much more fun than doing Medicine.

Omar's remarks may be partly post-results rationalisation but they also suggest the peer group has a disciplining, steering effect on individual choices. Institutional habitus in private schools like CB imposes a degree of conformity that makes it difficult to break out of narrowly defined parameters of acceptable choice.

The contrast with a large inner London state sixth form is obvious. Sharon, white, working class, talking about the attitude of her peer group in MU comments:

> I dunno, just go to the one you want, really. It's all very laid back. Everyone seems to be going all over the place.

Yet again we can see the ways in which the expressive order of the school impacts on higher education decision making. Schools like CB and HG have an institutional habitus informed by a stratified expressive order:

> Stratified schools were schools where the units of organisation were based on fixed attributes or attributes thought to be fixed e.g. age, gender, ability, categories of discourse (school subjects). It was thought that where unit/categories were considered fixed then the school would develop explicit horizontal and vertical structures. These would provide an unambiguous basis for the ritualisation of boundaries and the celebration of consensus. (Bernstein, 1996, p98)

In contrast, institutions like RC and MU have a far more differentiated expressive order, relayed through elaborated forms of personalised communication rather than through the intensive ritualisation common in stratified schools. One consequence in relation to higher education choice is, as Joely, a white working class student at MU indicates, 'we've all got our own sort of paths to go down. Everybody seems to be doing different things... Everyone just seems to get on with their own stuff'.

Concluding comments

Our research found little of the calculative, individualistic consumer rationalism that predominates in official texts (Ball, Macrae and Maguire, 1999). It was rare in CCS and FFCS, and was only one theme among many in MU and RU. While there were some highly organised choosers at both MU and RC, and, in particular, a number who could be described as active researchers, there were equally powerful themes of serendipity, intuitive response, narrow focus, directionlessness and making decisions on the hop in both institutions. Only in HG and CB do we find regular evidence of behaviour that approximates to objective calculative rationalism. Even here there would need to be qualifications because in a key sense many of these privileged students only need to follow their inclinations in order to achieve their goals (Bourdieu, 1990a). While both of these private schools provided protected worlds of 'already realised ends – procedures to follow, paths to take' (Bourdieu, 1990a) the state students in the two large sixth forms, unless they were recognised as Oxbridge material, were likely to be negotiating a morass of choices they often felt ill-equipped to deal with. Even more disadvantaged were the predominantly working class students in both CCS and FFCS involved in a process of finding out what you cannot have, what is not open for negotiation and then selecting from the few options left (Reay *et al*, 2002).

In spite of an inevitable degree of overlap and blurring of boundaries between peer group, family and institution we argue that there are specific effects from attending a particular educational institution. And these become most evident when examining the choices of similar kinds of students across the private-state divide. As we argued at the beginning of this chapter, higher education applicants are located within a complex matrix of influences which are best represented by overlapping circles of individual, family, friends and institution. The relative weight of these spheres of influence shift and change over time for students, generating an inevitable degree of overlap and blurring boundaries between peer group, family and institution. Within this messy confusion we have tried to disentangle some of the effects of institutional habitus and to indicate some of the ways in which it has an influence over and above the direct impact of family background.

We see our attempt to theorise a school effect as operating in a different dimension to the largely atheoretical work on school effectiveness, with its explicit political agenda around seeing teachers as both problem and solution. Instead, our work seeks to begin to unpick the dynamic relationships between schools and catchments in an analysis which tries to identify both the differences between schools and the difference those differences make, without detaching institutions from their wider social context. In this chapter we have tried to indicate the ways in which the various components of institutional habitus – educational status, organisational practices and the expressive order – influence student identities, the process and pattern of choice making and the range of higher education institutions chosen.

Yet within the same institution there is always a degree to which institutional habituses are mobilised differentially for different students. Furthermore, the dynamic between institutional habitus and catchment is inevitably going to be prone to misfirings in which the varying amounts of cultural capital students possess (individual effects) at times takes precedence over the collective effects of institutional habitus. In the next chapter we focus on parental involvement in student choices of higher education, examining the ways in which families and especially parents are involved in the processes of decision making about higher education. In particular, we utilise the concept of familial habitus to explore how differences in cultural, economic, social and academic capital impact on higher education choices (David *et al*, 2003).

4

Parents and higher education choice

This chapter explores parental involvement in students' choices of higher education in relation to gender, social class and ethnic issues. Recent research argues that 'parents are having an increasing impact on how candidates choose courses and institutions' (Tysome, 2004, p1). But as always the important questions to ask are: which parents? and in which ways are they becoming involved? We consider different aspects of involvement – interest, influence and support, investment and intrusion. Secondly, we provide case studies to illustrate both gender, class and ethnic differences and a range of parental approaches to the choice process. We include examples in which parents, and particularly mothers, are heavily involved, examples where parents express support but have little active involvement, and a number of cases in which tensions between parents and child arise in the choice process. These latter examples are mostly gendered, with boys resisting the involvement of mothers. But the data also reveals the ways in which gender is always mediated by social class. We draw on the notion of familial habitus – the deeply ingrained system of perspectives, experiences and predispositions family members share (Reay, 1998; David et al, 2003) – in order to make better sense of gendered and intra-class as well as inter-class differences in involvement.

An important aspect of familial habitus is the complicated compilation of values, attitudes and knowledge base that families possess in relation to the field of higher education. It is profoundly influenced by the educational experiences of parents and in our interview sample 41 per cent (50 out of 120 students) came from families where they were the first generation to go on to higher education; eight out of twelve in SCCS; twelve out of twenty-three in RC, nineteen out of twenty-three in FFEC and nine out of thirty-three in MU. In contrast, only two students in CB came from non-graduate family backgrounds and none in HG. The experience of higher education is qualitatively different for these 50 students compared with that of their 70 more educationally privileged counterparts. We would suggest that even when parents are in middle class jobs, if there is little or no experience of higher education such families are more insecurely positioned within the field of higher education than families where members have experience of university.

However, for a majority of the middle class families in the sample university attendance was taken for granted. Pat Allatt (1996) writes about the 'taken for granted assumptions' embedded in middle class family processes where the expectation of going to university does not need to be articulated. It is 'too true to warrant discussion' (Douglas, 1975, p3-4). We saw such assumptions over and over again in the middle class transcripts and draw on examples in this chapter. Familial habitus results in the tendency to acquire expectations that are adjusted to what is acceptable 'for people like us' (Bourdieu, 1984, p64-5). In relation to higher education Bourdieu and Passeron argue that:

> Depending on whether access to higher education is collectively felt, even in a diffuse way, as an impossible, possible, probable, normal or banal future, everything in the conduct of the families and the children (particularly their conduct and performance at school) will vary, because behaviour tends to be governed by what is 'reasonable' to accept. (Bourdieu and Passeron, 1977, p226)

A significant majority of middle class applicants in our study were engaging with higher education choice in contexts of certainty and entitlement. In this chapter we illustrate some of the ways in which such established middle class familial habituses generate the pursuit of advantage and the defence of distinction. We also examine the conscious application and hard work novitiate middle class families had to engage in. And as we see in chapter 5, middle class groupings were engaging in very different practices and processes, and operating in very different contexts to those of our working class students.

In this chapter we focus specifically on the perspective of parents on the choice process. However, our interviews with the 120 students also included a range of questions that asked about parental involvement and family dynamics of the choice process, so that data is also drawn on. Just as the student interview sample was predominantly middle class (79 out of 120) so was the parental interview sample (34 out of 40). The parental sample was skewed towards what we have called, in chapter 1, the established middle classes but other fractions of the middle classes were also represented. The six parents from working class families saw higher education as necessary because of the changes that they perceived in the labour market. One mother of a girl (Anne) from MU, and two fathers of sons (Stewart and Michael) from RC, although not having experienced higher education themselves, saw it as vitally important for their children's future success. Some parents had obtained professional qualifications that would now be part of higher education, such as teaching and accountancy, making them an intermediate middle class fraction. For example, Joshua's mother (RC; Black African) told us:

> I: If I remember correctly Joshua said that you attended university yourself
>
> J's Mum: He probably assumed that I did. I didn't. And the reason I didn't is because university was not really the right channel for me, to do my course, ...in my day, sometimes they beg you to come and take a job. I remember being begged to take computer training in Barclays Bank...and they would pay me the full amount, the full salary, and I would have full training and I wasn't interested, because I wasn't interested in computing. If I knew it was so money spinning now maybe I should have gone for it....

Joshua's mother illustrated how dramatic changes in higher education had been through her own biography. She, like almost all the parents we interviewed, saw higher education as axiomatic and automatic, whatever their own educational biography and choice of school. She also told us:

> I: ...just when in your mind did you begin to think about Joshua going to University?
>
> J's Mum: Oh, it's been on my mind all along that he's going
>
> I: Can I ask you why?
>
> J's Mum: Because it's very important, education is important and university gives him a good background to the next step in his career ... because if you attend university it gives you at least a leeway in comparison and gives you more opportunities when you get there, than those who are in job training...

For other middle class families there was no seamless process. Several students, mainly boys at state schools, had not wanted to involve their parents – particularly if they were not doing well at school. Will's mother (MU, white middle class) chided herself. Their son was laid back and resistant to the process, having messed up his UCAS form. She told us that they had not started the application process early enough despite the fact that she taught in an art college and her husband had been to Oxford:

> Well, when we first started to think about it? I suppose it was rather too late really. I suppose we did start to think about it at the beginning but we didn't quite realise, you know, how early we had to apply, you know, for universities and stuff. And neither did he ... He couldn't get it together to fill in the form, and he gave it to me so late, but by that time, the big thing really, that we didn't know, that we didn't realise, was his predicted grades had such an influence on, you know, the UCAS form. And how important the predicted grades were, if we'd known we'd have pushed him harder in his mocks, you know, or chivied him a bit more last year...

Thus gender and family dynamics played a part in forming expectations and the processes of choice-making irrespective of whether or not the parents had been in higher education themselves. A number of sons had a different version of the choice process – one which countered mothers' concerns of overly laid-back sons with accusations of pushy mothers:

> I can't deal with my mother telling me what to do -'do this, do that, do that, no that's not how to do it'. I can't handle it. I just can't deal with it and that's what happened with the UCAS form. I thought for God's sake leave me alone. (Rowan, MU)

In contrast to this picture of intense, directive involvement, it is primarily students from working class families who felt their parents lacked the competences required to engage constructively with the choice process (Reay, 1998; David *et al*, 2003):

> I did make the decisions on my own, 'God, it sounds like – yeah, my parents had nothing to do with it. I mean, they did, but the way I look at it, it sounds really terrible, but my parents, because the thing is my parents let me do what I want to do, it's not like they are letting me go wild, but they want me to choose what I want to choose. They haven't been to university themselves so they don't know a lot about which are the best places to go to. My dad says 'its just up to you' although my mum has got a bit of a bee in her bonnet but I still have a bit of independence and freedom. (Deirdre, white working class, MU)

Again, even here, the mother is a figure of significance with her 'bee in her bonnet'. Ms Keen, Head of the Sixth Form in the school with the most working class intake of the five making up the MU sixth form consortium, confirms that Deirdre's experience is a common one in her school:

> An awful lot of our parents haven't been to university themselves and they tend to leave it to their children to sort out, with help from the school of course. There's definitely no three way dialogue ... It's more a case of students informing their parents rather than asking them for advice.

And beyond working class parental unfamiliarity with the field of higher education, Fiona hints at the unsuitability of working class familial habitus for dealing with the process of higher education choice:

> All of us are very short-term people, we don't think about the future that much until it arrives. Which is good to some degree but not really in situations like sorting out university because you don't sort of get what you need to get done. (Fiona, Scottish working class student, MU)

This does not mean that middle class young people were regularly consulting their parents about higher education choices. They were not. Lesley Pugsley (1998) writes of how a number of young people in her study filter information about the higher education process, providing their parents with selective information, and there was a degree of filtering going on in our study. Rather, across the whole sample, the transition from the compulsory schooling stage to post 16 often involved a switch from middle class parents 'making their minds up' (Reay and Ball, 1998) to, at least, a semblance of young people making their own minds up. As one mother put it 'It's her decision really, we would listen and give advice rather than try and make her mind up for her'. Like the 16 to 19 year olds in Rudd and Evan's (1998, p51) study, 'very often these students asserted their individuality and talked in terms of making their own decisions, independent of the family, the peer group and other structural influences'. However, we need to set against parental assertions that they were mostly leaving it to their child, and young people's claims that they were making their own minds up, the influences of, in particular, established middle class habitus (and the institutional expectations and processes described in the previous chapter) which meant that some young people's minds had been made up long before the move to sixth form:

> I guess it was my parents who started me thinking about higher education because I've always known I was going to do that so that had to come from my parents but actually thinking about what course and which one, to go through it was probably partly school, partly my parents. (Anthony, white, middle class, CB)

Established middle class families, mostly located in the private sector, were engaging in processes of cultural reproduction that, despite at times appearing uncertain, shaky and prey to individual idiosyncrasies, nevertheless operate to ensure the reproduction of familial habitus:

> Choosing was probably a very unscientific process actually. My father went to Trinity Cambridge to do law and he was always very keen to show her Cambridge and his old college, which he did when she was probably about thirteen. And she fell in love with it. And she decided that was where she wanted to go.

Samantha gains her three A levels and takes up her place at Trinity, following in her grandfather's footsteps. A recent investigation by the Cambridge student newspaper found that 40 per cent of students at Cambridge had a family member who went to Oxbridge (Woodward, 2000). We can see here the enduring power of parental influences on middle class choices of higher education that Allatt (1993; 1996) describes, in which parents and other influential family members almost imperceptibly prepare for and shape children's higher education choices. 'The agents only have to follow the leanings of their habitus' (Bourdieu, 1984, p223). There was an enormous difference between such established middle class familial habituses in which going to university is part of a normal biography, simply part of what people like us do, and often too obvious to articulate, and working class familial habitus, characterised by uncertainty, unfamiliarity, lack of knowledge and often confusion in relation to the field of higher education. Mrs Mattison provides a classic example of the former:

> I: When did you first consider what Tim would do after finishing A levels?
>
> Mrs M: (laughs) Like when he was born. It's always been an expectation. I think it's always been implicit because the academic world is part of our life and very familiar to Tim. I just assumed he would go. I suppose it was just seen as natural.

Later, talking about the league tables, she asserts that Tim did not need to refer to them because:

> In a sense he just knew which the best ones were. And it wasn't the league tables. It's just the sense of the university, the location, the history and just a kind of knowing that people just do know what's good.

Here familial habitus is evident in its very inexplicitness. And we have a very clear articulation of established middle class habitus and what Bourdieu calls 'the paradox of natural distinction" in which,

> one of the privileges of the dominant, who move in their world as fish in water, resides in the fact that they need not engage in rational computation in order to reach the goals that best suit their interests. All they have to do is to follow their dispositions which, being adjusted to their positions, 'naturally' generate practices adjusted to the situation. (Bourdieu, 1990a, p108)

Such a sense of familiarity, naturalness and entitlement is miles away from the experience of Khalid's father:

> in our youth parents did not have attitudes to education, they had attitudes to work and you had to go out and earn money for your family as soon as possible. (Mr Adu, Bangladeshi, working class father, CCS)

While the privately educated students in both CB and HG were subtly, tacitly, yet still powerfully influenced by family dispositions and parental attitudes, the influence of parents for many of the state educated students appeared on the surface to be messier, conflictual and difficult to gauge, For instance, as we have indicated earlier and will touch on later in the chapter, for many of the working class students parental involvement was primarily affective – an emotional engagement with and support of the choice process – but an involvement that often stopped short of any active influence on decision making. Here again gender is salient, with mothers, especially, investing heavily emotionally in their children's futures (David *et al*, 2003).

A majority of the state educated young people denied any significant parental influence as opposed to involvement in their decision making. For example, of the 33 MU students we interviewed only five claimed that parental input had been helpful, three (two boys and one girl) citing their mother and two (one girl and one boy) their father. Six students (three girls and three boys) stated that parents had been actively unhelpful. One boy and one girl cited both parents, two boys and one of the girls their father, and the remaining girl her mother. This compares with the data from the fifteen girls we interviewed at HG, the private girls' school. Here five girls stated that parents had been particularly helpful (one father, three mothers and in one case both parents), while only two girls cite unhelpful parents (one mother and one father).

Although many of the state educated students in particular denied any significant influence of parents, familial habitus, like institutional habitus, clearly generated a context that shaped the parameters of choice for young people even when parents were perceived to be distanced from the process. In a small number of cases, almost all boys, parent and child presented starkly different versions of the choice process. Mrs Mattison tells us:

> Tim and I have worked this through together and I think that meant between us we've covered all the different angles. It's also been fascinating and stressful. But not, thank God, to the point of making him ill or us having a bad relationship, well, not falling out for long.

Here we get an impression of a collaborative, emotionally intense, if at times fractious, process. Tim, in contrast, presents a more individualised process, in which his mother is relegated 'to being quite helpful with my personal statement'. Mrs Mattison emphasises her influence and involvement:

> I thought he should go to three Open days. I'd have liked him to go to as many as he could but because of the pressures of GCSEs there really wasn't time so we went to Clare, St Johns and Emmanuel.

But in Tim's account his mother disappears altogether:

> Cambridge came up because of personal friends. I know people who have been to Cambridge or had been so I approached the school. I'd already decided that's what I wanted to do without talking to anyone at school so I went to Emmanuel, St Johns and Clare. I just asked around what colleges were good.

This is offered to underline just how opaque and multi-layered family dynamics in relation to higher education choice can be. In our readings of student and parent versions, as well as taking account of social class, we need to recognise the impact of both gender and the wider student peer group culture. In schools like MU it is uncool for young people, and in particular young men, to be seen to be still taking advice from their parents.

So one of the major factors we need to take into account in our reading of parent and student data is that many of our sample have reached the stage of separating out from their family of origin. Particularly for students who are moving away from home, the transition to higher education is a process of developing some autonomy and becoming more independent. This appears to impact on how they feel about the involvement of parents, which is often read as intrusion rather than support or presented as marginal. The struggle to develop a greater degree of independence and autonomy may entail a certain amount of denial about the extent to which parents have been influential or directive. Yet, in contrast to both what they wrote in the questionnaires and said in response to direct questions about parental involvement, the parent's opinions, attitudes, aspirations, and in some cases lack of aspiration, though muted, permeate the young people's transcripts. They talk about anxious mothers, proud fathers, parents who are diffident and ill-informed in relation to education, and those who are confident and well-informed. All these characteristics contribute to familial habitus and have an implicit impact on young people's choices.

Similarly, parental transcripts cannot be read too literally. They require a degree of delving and decoding:

> She'd quite like to apply to Oxford. I think it's completely up to her … to be perfectly honest I feel that, as it's got to this stage I don't think it's going to matter much where she goes. (Mrs Warner, mother of Charlotte, HG)

> I'm not involved in anything because you know they look at you as if you're an idiot and old and in the end when they're that age they are going to do what they want to. (Mrs Needham, mother of Melissa, HG)

Both mothers give the impression that their daughters are free to make their own minds up independently of family dispositions, pressures and influences. However later in the interview, Mrs Warner reveals that her brother-in-law is an Oxford don and that visits to Oxford university have been a regular part of Charlotte's childhood, while Mrs Needham admits 'I've brought them all up on Radio 4 and Parliament Today. The little one goes to bed by Radio 4. They are indoctrinated, I think, a bit'. As we argued earlier, it is such taken for granted, barely perceptible aspects of familial habitus that shape decision making among the established middle classes.

Working class decision making is quite different. For Stuart's father:

> Where Stuart will go is based on finance. Basically the courses he's looking at were related to home and to his part-time job.

Here we are presented with starkly different criteria and parameters of choice to those articulated by established middle class parents like Mrs Warner and Mrs Needham. Stuart's choice is governed by the need to live at home and continue to work in his current job. However, for Stuart, Melissa and Charlotte choices are closed down to a handful of universities at most. For Stuart the process is constrained by economic realities. For Charlotte and Melissa it is the pursuit of distinction that is foremost, although this is no process of striving or struggle but rather one of ease and naturalness. As Bourdieu (1990b, p11) argues:

> To strive for distinction is the opposite of distinction: firstly because it involves recognition of a lack and a disavowal of a self-seeking aspiration, and secondly because, as can easily be seen ... consciousness and reflexivity are both cause and symptom of the failure of immediate adaptation to the situation which defines the virtuoso.

The established middle classes are the virtuosos of university choice. It is the less established fractions of the middle classes, those termed in chapter 1 the novitiate and intermediate middle classes, that increasingly have to put real effort into the choice process and in doing so reveal their relative lack of distinction. It is important to recognise that this process of striving has been compounded by the move from an elite to a mass system. Middle class fractions, apart from the most privileged, have been affected by the influx of the working classes and the routine non manual middle classes (those with no immediate family history of HE) into higher education. In order to keep their distance from the newcomers, our novitiate middle class graduates have had to intensify the time, effort and money they invest in education. However, while the less established middle class groupings strive in relation to the field of higher education, as we see in the next chapter, the working classes struggle and risk a habitus divided against itself (Bourdieu, 1999).

We would not wish to convey the impression, however, that familial habitus tells the entire story of higher education choice-making. Sometimes there are glitches and ruptures in what should be a seamless veneer and deliberate interventions are then called for. In particular, as we saw in the example of laid-back Will, the idiosyncacies and vagaries of personality are ill-explained in Bourdieu's theoretical framework. Mrs Seifert, whose eldest daughter 'just knew Cambridge was where she wanted to go', provides an example of an established middle class mother who, confronted by a second daughter who is 'a free spirit and a bit of a rebel', has to switch from gentle, barely perceptible steering to active involvement:

> I've not wanted to be too controlling or interfering because Helena is very resistant to that. So I kept on being a bit worried throughout but kept at a distance ... Helena resents parental influence much more than some kids do.

However, when Helena decides on Newcastle as one of her choices, Mrs Seifert decides she needs to become more proactive. Here also Mrs Seifert's sense of distinction in relation to suitable and unsuitable universities for a child like hers, becomes explicit:

> This was typical, this bravado...you know she could go to a second rate university, it didn't matter. It was quite clear she was choosing her university in a way that I thought she would go somewhere and wouldn't be stretched. And then I started getting really concerned ... Then I decided I would have to intervene. And I would have to think of a way of intervening.

Mrs Seifert's ploy is not to offer advice herself but to find other people whom Helena respects to speak to her:

> Firstly a very very good friend of mine who I studied with originally who then did English at Oxford. And he came to stay one weekend and he started telling me that if Helena applied to particular universities where there is say a very large mixed student intake she wouldn't necessarily find a group of people of her calibre or her interests. And he started coming out with all these other sort of insider comments about different departments and how English is taught. So I said 'please talk to Helena about it' so they had this sort of hour where she listened to him so that was very useful. And then what I did was I went on the internet and started printing out syllabuses from different English departments. And just sort of handed them to her and she suddenly realised that the same discipline at different universities is totally different. And there were some where the requirements for getting in were beyond the realms of consideration. And then I was very relieved and I could see she wasn't an Oxford sort of person and I went on the Oxford College sites and some of them said 'Oh it's great fun, you dress up in academic gowns and walk backwards' – and I thought Helena will never stand for this. Then I did the same for Cambridge and narrowed my choice to two Colleges which looked as if she would actually enjoy being there. It was the ethos. St Catherine's the one she's applied to. It said they had a very strong student drama and theatre club. It seemed so Helena.

In Mrs Seifert's tale, as well as 'the tacit recognitions of class embedded in social relations' (Bottero and Irwin, 2003: 472), we can see a particular kind of social capital. This, perhaps more aptly named academic social capital, allows the established middle classes to equip their children with the types of contacts that permit them access to elite universities (Ball, 2003; Savage, 2003; Devine,

2004). However, apart from the extensive academic social capital reveals, the quotation also demonstrates that even established middle class parents occasionally need to engage in repair work. Here we have an established middle class mother confronted by a daughter who is 'a bit of a rebel', 'very left wing for her private girls school', and at risk of making a choice that goes against the grain of the familial habitus – who might end up 'going to a second rate university'. However, her mother's carefully considered intervention corrects the situation. 'The distances that need to be kept' (Bourdieu, 1984, p472) are maintained. But not through the operations of the pre-reflexive, unconscious habitus featured in much of Bourdieu's writing, but through calculation and foresight; a much more strategic deliberation aimed at maintaining the requisite social distances and distinctions. Helena, like her older sister, goes to Cambridge, but unlike her sister, who went to a very traditional Cambridge College, Helena, at her mother's behest, applies to St Catherine's, where there is a better match with her creative, rather rebellious, left wing persona.

So, although for much of the time, in established middle class familial habituses we see different structures of perception, appreciation and action to those evident among less established middle class groupings, occasionally there are misfirings that require more deliberate intervention. We also glimpse evidence of the established middle class awareness of subtle differences, not just between elite universities but even between colleges within them, reflecting the complicated and differential nature of the English middle classes and the endless variety of social types that the educational system is capable of producing and reproducing (Power *et al*, 2003).

Gender differences in involvement

Unlike most of the existing research, which suggests that fathers play a greater role in their offspring's education as they grow older (David *et al*, 1994; Pugsley, 1998), this study indicates that fathers were less involved than mothers although, as we discuss later, there were exceptions (see also Brooks, 2004). Three African fathers took a highly interventionist role in their daughters' choices, while two divorced fathers were adamant that they wanted their sons to go to particular elite universities. However, the general tendency was for athers to be less involved than mothers. In particular, working class fathers were evidently starting from a very low base:

> It's only now that I think my dad is getting interested in my education. Before, he wasn't really. He didn't get involved if I was doing something. I don't even think he ... I would give him my report or something and he'd go – huh. That was about it – huh, good. It's only when I do something bad that he goes – what? takes any notice. (Fiona, Scottish working class, MU)

and:

> I mean, my dad has always been very, I've never really had that much feedback from my dad. So it's – oh yeah, well done. And that's it and that's never been enough for me. And he's still like that today. He'd rather criticise me than actually... (Inka, working class FE Student mixed English/German parentage)

Eric, a Black access student in his early twenties, refers to a disagreement between himself and his father in which they have reached an impasse and so no longer discuss Eric's plans to study:

> I mean, he does want me to further my education but he sort of thinks that because I've not done what he wants me to do then you know, it's not going to be the right thing for me, or maybe I'm not going to progress in it, or maybe I'm gonna give up halfway. He sort of, he's not optimistic about my future really on account of me not doing what he wants so we don't talk about it anymore.

Although none of the other parent child relationships appear to have become so entrenched, a number of other students hint at previous areas of conflict:

> I knew about sociology and I wanted to do it and it's my decision. And whether they like it or not, I mean, my mum is coming to accept it now. And if she didn't like it she'd just have to accept it because it's what I'm going to do and she can't change my view or anything. But she does support me and she does see now that you want to do something you enjoy, that it's really important to study something you're going to enjoy. (Deirdre, Irish working class, MU)

As Lesley Pugsley found, 'some young people choose to make their own decisions at this level of choice, often bypassing parents, many of whom are recognised as ill-equipped to engage with the discourses of the higher education market' (Pugsley, 1998, p85).

Social class is again key. It is parents with no history of high education themselves who are primarily seen as unable to make a contribution. General expectations could be circumvented in the formalities of choosing. Alomgir expresses a common attitude among young people from families with no history of higher education attendance:

> I don't really get my family involved, I just get on with my stuff basically. They don't know anything about it so there's not much point talking to them about it.

Eric, Deirdre and Shuma all end up doing what they, rather than their parents, want, as Deidre's comment highlights:

> And even my mum, you know. She's been interested throughout, giving me advice and stuff – not that I've taken it.

Most of the students who were the first generation in their family to apply to university, (in particular, the nineteen FE students, the seven Bangladeshi and three Chinese students) presented both their parents as peripheral to the higher education choice process, although Shuma mentioned her father's negative involvement and the three Chinese students said that their parents and other family members were intending to contribute to university costs.

When parents were described as supportive, it was mostly said about mothers, although sometimes, as in Sarah's case, parents' involvement was tolerated rather than welcomed, and portrayed as not particularly useful:

> My mum has been supportive and everything, she's like, she's asking about the courses and she's offered to come up with me to the open days and everything, but I said it would be better if I went alone. I'm going with some friends. My mum and I would be looking for totally different things I think whereas with my friends I know we'll be looking at the same things... My mum will be wanting to make sure I'm safe like is there good security in the accommodation. I mean that is important but I want to check out the facilities and stuff. (Sarah, dual heritage, working class student, MU)

Working class mothers could be seen as unnecessarily overprotective of their daughters. Collette, Sarah, Deirdre and Aba all talk about the struggle they have had to convince their mothers it is a good idea to leave home:

My mum just wants me to stay somewhere in London. I don't think she cares where I go as long as I stay at home. (Aba)

To set against the binary of over-solicitous mothers and less involved fathers, we also found an altogether different model of parental involvement by some of the private school students. Henry's father has accompanied him on a number of university visits and Henry portrays his involvement, and that of his mother, as both welcome and supportive:

My parents have helped me a great deal, they were initially the people who convinced me to go and ask the school whether I might apply to Oxbridge, and they initially, they took me around the town. My father took off a lot of time so he and I could visit all the towns and universities I was going to. Drive around them and find out about the atmosphere of the city.

Like the young men in Rachel Brooks' study (2004), Frank and Ben have also had a good deal of guidance from fathers, which they perceive as positive and helpful. However, Henry's experience of positive parental guidance was by no means the norm at CB. In Edward's case paternal input appears to be very directive:

And until last year my dad was very set on me going to Oxford. He went there and he wanted me to go there.

However, the two boys in the sample from uncredentialled business backgrounds, who are on assisted places, find themselves in similar positions to the working class students whose parents' lack of cultural and academic social capital results in their making little contribution to the choice process other than general emotional support:

They haven't been. It's only because they haven't been themselves, so it would be wrong for me to expect them to be able to help me. They wouldn't really be able to help me in terms of universities, simply because they haven't gone. But they keep telling me to go, and apart from that they can't help me that much, I don't think. (Omar)

Even when parents do possess the requisite cultural and academic social capital, their children still often view their involvement as something which would impinge on their independence:

> They're not particularly involved. I'm quite independent. middle class Indian student, CB)

Or it is simply irrelevant to the process:

> I think they said if you want any help just ask, but I don't think I ended up asking them for help anyway, but they were there if I wanted them, yeah. (Duncan, white middle class student, CB)

The most striking exception to the binary of highly involved mothers and more distant fathers is the experience of the three African girls at CCS who were the only state educated students to speak of fathers extensively involved in processes of guiding and channelling:

> And then I spoke to my dad and he said it was not really a good sort of career, not really steady, so we talked through that and said I must do something which I could always set myself up in in the future. Where there was a good future, a steady career. So we talked through subjects and things I was good at and decided to do sort of law and business. (Temi)

> I wouldn't want my dad to come. I would take my older brother or my sister... Probably my dad would be looking for different things. I know he would. Is there a church? That's the first thing he'll look for. Which will be a thing I look for as well, because most of them do have Christian Societies, but he would look for a lot of things, you know, he would just look at things like that whereas I'll be looking for other things as well. (Sara)

Temi, Deborah and Sara all have fathers with degree level education and although Sara talks about trying to limit her father's involvement, his encouragement and guidance in relation to higher education choice is a constant throughout her secondary schooling:

> So I said – yeah, I want to be a lawyer. And then I did a little bit of reading, you know, my dad showed me a few things in the encyclopaedia and then he helped me find some stuff about it. I read it and from then on it was just lawyer, lawyer, lawyer ... I was quite firm about the ones I wanted to go to because I did do some research before. So it was kind of helpful in telling me what to look for. but my dad had already told me a lot of that stuff. (Sara)

However, for all three paternal involvement leads to a degree of conflict:

At the end of the day I would have ended up doing what I wanted to do, but it was just him trying to kind of get on my nerves, sort of thing. It was him trying to sort of get me to do what he wanted me to do, but he always knew I was going to do what I wanted to do and he was always going to accept that in the end. But because I had been harping on and on and on about being a lawyer and everything and all of a sudden I woke up one day and said I wanted to be a physiotherapist he was quite shocked, but by the end he didn't really mind. (Deborah)

and:

At first my dad was just like – do law and that's it. I said – no I'm not. Yes you are. No I'm not and we argued about it. And mum was like – well, maybe she could keep her options open, because doing a straight law degree won't enable me to do different types of jobs. If it is business related then my options are a lot more open, OK, because I don't particularly want to be a lawyer. I don't mind being a legal advisor or something like that, but I don't want to be a lawyer... My mum and I persuaded him it was alright. I think in the back of his mind he thinks – she'll do a law business degree and then I'll send her to Nigeria to do a two year law course. (Temi)

Rachel Brooks (2002, p219) points out that although existing research reveals that parents 'may be the most widely consulted source of information and advice, they are not necessarily the most useful'. And this was certainly the perspective of most of the young people in our study. However, as we have glimpsed throughout the accounts of both parents and their children, despite the denials of many young people, even when they were not having a direct influence, parents and families exerted powerful indirect influences that delineated the field of possible choices (David, 1993; David *et al*, 1996). Even in those cases where either there was not an apparent direct parental engagement with the choice process or parent and child were in conflict, familial habitus and family resources of cultural, social and academic capital continued to have an overwhelming influence 'in the absence of any deliberate inculcation' (Bourdieu and Boltanski, 2000, p18).

Synchronised or out-of-step? The relationship between familial and institutional habituses

In the last chapter we discussed the influence of institutional habitus, arguing that there were specific effects arising from attending a particular educational establishment, whilst recognising tha. in many instances, there is a degree of overlap and blurring of boundaries between family and educational establishment. Here we examine more closely the dynamics of the relationship between familial and institutional habituses. Pugsley (1998) argues that in her study the schools played a crucial role in providing information and facilitating the transition to university. However, there is perhaps too much separation of institutional from familial habituses in her analysis and thus too little recognition of the ways in which institutional habituses develop out of the social and cultural characteristics of their intakes. Rather, we would argue that there is a continual synergy between institutional and familial habituses. The thrusting practices that constitute careers advice in CB are powerfully influenced by the economic, cultural and social capitals and practices of students and their families. As the narrative of Dr Anderson, head of careers, indicates at various points, parental expectations shaped the format of advice offered. In particular, parental and peer group pressure was instrumental in maintaining the school's concentration on access to elite universities, in particular Oxbridge, despite Dr Anderson's own feelings that greater consideration should be given to a wider range of institutions:

> I think we have a real problem in that parents, or the students, don't appreciate that some of the universities that may be newer and are further down the formal league table have some excellent vocational courses and produce students who have high employability. Quite a lot of parents would prefer their child to go to what they see as a good university, and might actually come out with employability prospects which are lower than if they had gone to a university that was perhaps not quite so high up in the league table. Getting over the idea that a university might be low down in the league table but have some real specialisms which are very, very good is difficult to sell. And that is a real problem with the boys who get hold of this idea, in part I feel from their parents, whose experience of university is fifteen, twenty years out of date.

So we can see that, even in CB, there is no seamless flow between the dominant familial habitus among students and institutional habitus. Beneath a veneer of harmony there are still disjunctures and ruptures where inconsistencies and disagreements can occur. As Dr Anderson confirms, most students at CB come from estaɔlished middle class families with parents working in business and the private sector. In contrast, many of the families whose children go to MU, although members of the established middle class, could be seen to be part of Bernstein's 'new middle class' (Bernstein, 1975; 1996) in the sense that they are predominantly public sector professionals occupied in the production and distribution of symbolic knowledge. The conflict the latter group experience in relation to the balance between guidance and allowing their children freedom and autonomy is evident in the following fieldnotes on a parents' meeting at MU:

> One of the fathers came back to the issue of autonomy and the discussion became far more animated. He said he was increasingly concerned about the excess of freedom his daughter was given in the sixth form, stating 'Of course freedom and autonomy are important' (lots of nodding from other parents) but as far as he was concerned, MU hadn't got the right balance between freedom and support/guidance. One consequence was that by encouraging autonomy and treating his 17 year old daughter like an adult, the school was also encouraging her to ignore and/or devalue his advice and experience. At this lots of other parents joined in, all agreeing that they too had the same concern. Although there were lots of positive comments validating MU's approach and a consensus developed that the ethos of MU inculcates a semblance of independence and maturity in students which appears to be very positive for the young people, most parents acknowledged as negative the encouragement students were frequently given to believe they are old/mature enough to make their own decisions. A number of mothers argued that their own child often felt there was no need to supply parents with information, let alone ask for advice. MU was perceived to be colluding in this by operating as if their responsibility and relationship was with the student alone rather than being one which included the student's family.

Here we can see again how institutional habitus can sometimes be slightly out of step with the dominant familial habitus among a school's students and parents; that although there is a close relationship between the two, as McDonough (1997) asserts, there is also space for a degree of fluidity, of moving beyond or falling behind. Perhaps we also glimpse here the tensions within 'the new middle class' in relation to the virtues of visible and invisible pedagogic regimes (Bernstein, 1975; 1996).

The dissonance articulated at the meeting, with its undercurrent ambivalence and a degree of angst, reveals aspects of the expressive order, a key element of institutional habitus. The parents at the meeting, the vast majority of whom were new middle class professionals, including academics, social workers, teachers, psychologists, health workers, local authority executives and media workers, were all unanimous that, as one parent stated, 'freedom and autonomy were important'. They all also agreed that the decision lay with their child; that they and the school were only there to advise, not impose. The difficulty for many of them was that they felt the school was giving out a message that choice making was totally the province of the young person, that adult guidance was unimportant, whereas, as another parent pointed out at the meeting 'We'd just like our kids to recognise that grown ups might have something relevant to say'.

This episode suggests a number of interesting connections. First, whilst recognising an inevitable degree of incongruence between familial and institutional habitus across all six institutions, when we focus on the dominant familial habitus there seem to be important links between, on the one hand, the institutional habitus of the private schools and the 'old middle classes', (Bernstein, 1975; 1996) and between the institutional habitus of progressive inner city comprehensives like MU and different fractions of the 'new middle classes' as Bernstein (1975; 1996) suggests. Second, and connectedly, the episode tells us something about the expressive order of MU and a key way in which it differs from the two private schools where the importance of adult guidance, although more commonly in the form of staff rather than parents, is taken for granted; it is beyond discussion. The expressive order in the private schools is stratified, with strongly positioned teacher-student relationships of control. In MU, and also RC, the expressive order appears to be less hierarchically ordered, teacher-student relationships are much more fluid, with more opportunities for student self governance and autonomy.

These differences in expressive order are played out in higher education decision making in the institutions. While adult guidance is taken for granted in HG and CB, there is a much stronger peer group culture of marginalising adult advice, particularly that of rents, in both RC and MU. Although there is a sprinkling of helpful parents and other adults in young people's narratives, the expressive order, particularly at MU, is characterised by a collective view that the decision is primarily the young person's. At the same time we have tried to convey the subtle, tacit ways in which middle class familial reproduction is defended and ensured.

Concluding comments

In this chapter we have examined parental involvement in higher education through the lens of familial habitus, focusing in particular on the class differences that emerge. We have also examined gender differences in relation to both parents and students. In the next chapter we focus on working class young and mature students. Our emphasis is on individual effects and the impact of cultural capital, or rather lack of 'legitimate cultural capital' (Bourdieu, 1984). Just as we have drawn out intra-middle class differences in this chapter, we examine differentation and difference within working class groupings in the next.

5
Working class students

This chapter concentrates on the higher education choice processes of a specific segment of higher education applicants; young and mature working class students who as recently as ten years ago would have been unlikely to apply to university. It explores how the students negotiate the process and attempts to understand the meanings they ascribe to higher education, and, specifically, the divisions within it. Through the students' accounts, the chapter examines various mechanisms of social closure which operate to reproduce existing inequalities within the higher education sector. It also explores intra-working class differences, arguing that there are different working class fractions with differing priorities in relation to risk, challenge and fitting in. The chapter concludes by challenging political discourses which position widening access and the advent of a mass system of higher education as unproblematically positive advances.

Widening participation in higher education has become a Government mantra over recent years. The UK Government policy is to attract increasing numbers of non-traditional applicants to higher education. However, the statistics suggest that recent policy changes have made it more rather than less difficult for some non-traditional students to attend university (Callender, 2003b; Blanden and Machin, 2003). In this chapter we focus on the psychological and sociological aspects of the higher education choice process, arguing that class subjectivity and particularly issues around belonging, fitting in and feelings of authenticity are key to understanding working class experiences of the move into higher education.

Louise Archer and Merryn Hutchings (2001) in their study of working class non-participants in higher education, describe working class young people as positioning themselves outside of higher education. The respondents in their study constructed higher education as a white middle class place, placing themselves as 'potentially able to take advantage of the benefits it can offer, but not as owners of it'. Furthermore, the accounts of the young people in their study were strongly mediated by concerns about risk and cost. Risks and costs which were financial but also personal. It is important to remind ourselves that the link between class and education, in which failure is emblematic of the working class relationship to schooling, frequently makes working class transitions to higher education complex and difficult.

Our working class sample of 41 were all located in the state sector and were diverse in terms of ethnicity, gender and age. Almost half were located in the FE College with seventeen students from British black and white manual working class backgrounds, most of whom were currently employed or had been employed in low status white collar work in the public or service sector. The range of work undertaken included routine office work, childcare assistant, street trader, barmaid, shop assistant and youth worker. Two were from self-employed backgrounds. Lesley's father managed a small jewellery shop where her mother worked as a shop assistant. Her current partner is also self employed and runs his own sign writing business. Darren's father is a small property developer, although Darren works as a security guard. Both, however, self-identified as working class. Both, in common with the other seventeen, were the first in their families to aim for university, were on low incomes and living in public sector households. Accordingly, we have included them in our working class sample, while attempting to address the ambiguity of their situation. Thus some of our sample are already mobile, located in intermediate middle class positions or, in Bourdieu's terms, petit-bourgeois.

A further critical mass of working class students were located CCS, the predominantly ethnic minority, working class inner cit. comprehensive. Here eight of the twelve young people were working class, mainly Bangladeshi but including one Chinese and one Irish young man. In MU there were nine working class students, eight girls and one Chinese young man. In RU we located five working class students, three female and two male. Our sample has a gender imbalance, with twenty-six females and fifteen males. One of us (Diane Reay) did attempt to access working class students in the private boys' school but was told rather embarrassedly by the Head of Careers that 'that would be difficult as that is not the sort of background our students come from'. We deliberately set out to interview as many working class applicants as possible, so the proportion of working class students in our interview sample (a third of the total) does not represent the overall class balance in the four state institutions in our research study. Although the main focus of this chapter is social class, ethnicity and gender are recognised and discussed as mediating factors throughout.

'Doing the best I can with the little I've got': material constraints on choice

The official and academic discourses that assume we should all develop personalised educational projects for self improvement rarely recognise the material exigencies that bear down on the lives of the poor. As is evident in the quotations below, that is how many of the working class students saw themselves. While recent major studies of the transitions made by 16 to 19 year olds found that young people had a strong sense of having a variety of choices (Chisholm, 1995; Brynner *et al*, 1997; Du Bois-Reymond, 1998; Ball *et al*, 2000), this was not the case for the majority of working class students in our study. Choice for a majority involved either a process of finding out what you cannot have, what is not open for negotiation and then looking at the few options left, or a process of self-exclusion. One working class student claimed to have 'a choice of one'. Material circumstances meant that a majority were operating within narrow circumscribed spaces of choice, in which the location of a university becomes crucial. Khalid is an extreme example of working class localism, but most of the working class

...dents felt geographically constrained, as the quotes below ...dicate:

> You see City University is a walking distance from my home, Westminister is also walking distance, but it's not that short as it is to City University. So I'm sort of still thinking. (Khalid, Bangladeshi working class student, CCS)

> Distance is very important. It's got to be an easy journey, somewhere I can cycle to is great'. (Rick, white working class)

> Distance is the most important thing. It's almost bound to be when you've got three young kids. (Maggie, white working class lone mother)

> I: How did you choose the universities?

> Andy: Well first of all they're all near.

> The location is really the most important thing because there is a course in Birmingham and I can't go there so it is no use for me. It just gives me heartache, finding something really interesting and I can't go there. (Rumana, working class eastern European refugee)

So geography determines choice for a majority of working class students. Steve explains that the only higher education institution he has put down on his UCAS form is Roehampton because 'there is nothing else that seemed to make sense in terms of working and travelling', while Alomgir told us 'I need to go to my local university because my studies need to fit in with my work and family commitments'. The material constraints under which many of these students were struggling meant that the cost of travel and accommodation were primary considerations. Only nine of our 41 working class students (23%) were considering moving out of the family home to attend university, in contrast to over 70 per cent of the middle class students (see also Holdsworth, 2005).

Archer and Hutchings (2001, p561) found that their working class respondents perceived the move into higher education as mediated by risks and costs, 'applying and getting to university was talked about as an uncertain (risky) process which would cost considerable time'. As is evident throughout this chapter, the transition to higher education was similarly risky for the working class students in our study. Their narratives provide glimpses of the actual social processes underpinning recent statistics (O'Leary, 2000; UC. 2000; Galindo-Rueda *et al*, 2004); narratives in which both ri and costs are foregrounded.

Counting the costs: working class students and labour market participation

Choice of higher education is constrained by the predicted and actual A-level grades achieved by the students. A-level achievement (and subsequent performance at university) is affected by a range of factors. One factor is clearly the time available for and devoted to study. Students from both white and ethnic minority working class families were much more likely than their more affluent counterparts to be working long hours in the labour market and to envisage having to continue to do so while studying for a degree (see also Payne, 2003).

Across our questionnaire sample of 502, a third of the students from the established middle classes were in paid employment compared with two thirds of students from working class households. In all, two-thirds of the state school students were working, less than a third of the private school students and 40 per cent of the mature students. Only one private school student was working more than 15 hours. Those working over 10 hours a week were also concentrated at the lower end of the socio-economic scale. Amongst the established middle classes only 10 per cent were working more than 10 hours, 17 per cent of the traditional middle classes, 21 per cent of the routine non-manual, 30 per cent of III M and 31 per cent of the unskilled. Not surprisingly there was a strong inverse link between number of hours worked and number of hours devoted to homework. In addition we can note that 41 (15%) students reported having extra tuition, over one quarter of private school students did so, less than 10 per cent of state school students, and one Access student.

Such practices make the possibility of attaining grades which would make elite universities a realistic goal easy for some and far more difficult for others. The qualitative data shed further light on this. Shaun (CCS), who was predicted an A and two C grades at A level, and had been hoping to go to Sussex to study Sociology, was despairing about his chances of success:

> It's all gone wrong for me. Because I've been getting no help from home I've had to find the money for rent, food, everything basically and there's no way I can get the work done anymore. I'm too exhausted. (Shaun, Irish working class, CCS)

and:

> I started to work for Safeways, and it has had a big effect on my education, because mostly I say I am coping, but what really happens is you are kidding yourself, when you say you are coping, because you are not, there is so much to do. (Khalid, Bangladeshi working class, CCS)

Fiona's text highlights the impossibility of pursuing a programme of four A levels which is increasingly common within the private sector, but from which working class students like herself are excluded because of the exigences of their economic circumstances:

> And then I started at Marks and Spencers and I was doing four days a week and trying to juggle four A levels ... And the four days in Marks and Spencers, even three A levels is impossible with all that other work. (Fiona, Scottish working class, MU)

Fiona eventually drops her fourth A level. While three of the thirteen boys interviewed at CB were studying four A levels, none of the other state educated students in the qualitative sample were studying more than three A levels, and three of the working class boys at CCS were only studying two. We can see here how structural influences, by constraining poorer students' range of options, operate to maintain hierarchies of distinction and differentiation within the field of higher education.

Exclusionary processes also operate within the field of higher education itself, with far more working class than middle class students talking about undertaking paid employment in both term time and the vacations while studying for a degree. Only two, out of a total of thirteen, CB boys contemplated undertaking paid work during term time when at university. A further two thought they might have to work in the holidays. Only three were working currently. In contrast, fourteen of the nineteen working class FE students were currently working and all but two said they would need to work while doing their degree. At CCS, all the working class young people were working currently and all anticipated working when at university. At MU, five out of the nine working class students had part-time employment, although all the working class students had worked throughout the lower sixth, and six expected to undertake paid work at degree level. Rick, a white working class FE student, while perhaps stating an extreme case, sums up a collective conundrum for working class students currently contemplating higher education:

> Not much of a choice really, it's either poverty or failure, cos I think having to work three days a week won't leave enough time to do the right amount of studying, and anyway if I'm in it for the experience of learning new things I need time to be able to do that ... to get some enjoyment out of it so I guess it's poverty. (Rick, white working class student, FFEC)

The importance of paid employment for the working class students, its centrality in their lives, meant it sometimes had an impact on choice that rarely emerged in the transcripts of young people from established middle class families.

Having to undertake paid work is only part of the problem. Other consequences for working class students of inadequate finances is that they cannot afford travel, decent accommodation or even essential course materials:

> I cried about my financial difficulties in class this morning because it is too much. It is very very difficult financially. Sometimes I need to go to the library but I don't want to walk and honestly I don't have the bus fare to go and so it is really affecting my studies at the moment because I can't afford to do anything and you think the course will not cost any money but then you need books and pens and writing paper. (Rumana, working class, eastern European refugee)

This was not just an issue for the mature students. The young working class male Bangladeshi students all spoke about their financial responsibilities to their families, while Shaun, a young Irish working class man, was living independently and trying to subsist on the income from three part-time jobs.

While the most pressing costs for working class students were financial we also need to recognise the other costs involved in the move into higher education. Many students were juggling extensive labour market commitments and domestic responsibilities with studying. This was particularly the case for the mature women students. In such circumstances any sort of social life is often sacrificed. Mature working class women students were often suffering from time poverty as well as financial poverty:

> It's not just the distance it's the time it takes to get there. I went down there for an interview and it took me over an hour and a half to get there and I just thought this is unrealistic because I am just going to feel every morning that I don't want to go. It's going to take forever just getting there and back. (Angie, working class dual heritage, lone mother)

> One of the reasons I chose London Metropolitan, although it's still probably 50 minutes to an hour to get there, is it's very direct for me because the Piccadilly line is at the end of my street so I can get on the tube and sit on it and just go down there so it is by far the easiest journey. (Maggie, white working class lone mother)

In particular, for mature working class women students the addition of family, and often child care, commitments rendered the idea of a student lifestyle, with its combination of independence, dependence, leisure and academic work, unthinkable. Being a student for them meant something entirely different from the conceptions and experiences of the younger, more privileged students:

> I have to be pragmatic. Can I drop Josh off at school and can I get a bus? (Carly, white working class lone mother)

Here we glimpse a further kind of time poverty; time for care of the self:

> Leisure is to go to the library. I watch a bit of TV but that is all the leisure there is time for. I've stopped everything else. (Rumana, working class eastern European refugee)

> I don't really find I have any time for myself now, but I know that even when I go to uni I am going to have the same problem. I've got to get used to not going out. (Denise, black working class lone mother)

One way of thinking about what is going on here is that these students are eschewing various aspects of a normal biography – social life, financial security and family relationships – in an attempt to respond to the demands of reflexive modernisation. Processes of reflexive modernisation call for 'a vigorous model of action in everyday life which puts the ego at its centre, allots and opens up opportunities for action to it' (Beck, 1992, p136). As Beck recognises, there are psychological costs in any project of putting the ego at the centre. These costs – guilt, anxiety and feelings of personal inadequacy – were particularly evident in the narratives of mature women students who were mothers.

The lone mothers at the FE college constituted a critical mass of students who were unable to move on to higher education at the end of the access course. A whole range of factors including prior qualifications, earlier educational experiences and levels of confidence may be implicated, but equally salient seems to be these women's inability to immerse themselves totally in their studies until all their domestic and child care responsibilities had been discharged.

'What's a person like me going to do at a place like that?' Knowing one's academic place

Bourdieu writes of how objective limits become transformed into a practical anticipation of objective limits; a sense of one's place which leads one to exclude oneself from places from which one is excluded (Bourdieu, 1984, p471). Mick (FFEC), who describes himself as white working class, has rejected the more elite universities like King's College London because, as he asserts, 'what's a person like me going to do at a place like that' and says that he would find 'going somewhere like King's daunting'. Despite what the league tables say, Roehampton is a good university for Mick because, after a negative experience of schooling, his priority is to go to an institution where he is comfortable, somewhere where there is a chance he will feel at home within education. Many of the working class students, particularly those on the Access courses, echo similar sentiments:

> Sally: I wasn't bothered about the league tables because I already knew where I wanted to go and I knew it was a good place.
>
> I: Good in the sense of...?
>
> Sally: Well, that it's the right place for me.

Here Sally exhibits a Bourdieurian sense of place: of 'one's relationship to the world and one's proper place within it' (Bourdieu, 1984, p474). For working class students like Sally and, to an extent Mick, university league tables are often an irrelevance. As Bourdieu and Passeron point out, in relation to access to higher education, choices are governed by what it is 'reasonable to expect' (Bourdieu and Passeron, 1977, p226), and both Sally and Mick have developed expectations that are acceptable for people like us (Bourdieu, 1990a).

The transcripts highlight the importance of students' psychological, as well as their financial and academic, proximity to different universities. For some students, one particular university is definitely where they want to be:

> Once I had been there I just knew. I will be really upset if I don't get the grades which I need because now I can't really imagine going anywhere else. (Anthony, white middle class, CB)

> I just liked the feel, you know, when you just walk in somewhere and think, I could be happy here. (Carly, white working class FE student)

While the privately educated students' sense of belonging is attached predominantly to elite universities such as Oxford and Cambridge, and the middle class state educated students articulated a sense of belonging primarily in relation to pre-1992 red brick universities, the working class students, with only one or two exceptions, spoke of a sense of belonging in relation to new universities. However, this sense of knowing their right place was sometimes cross-cut by barely acknowledged desires for more elite spaces. This brings us back powerfully to an issue raised in chapter 2: while students are clearly channelled towards some universities rather than others on the basis of exam predictions, choice of university is also a matter of taste and lifestyle in which social class is a key determinant of choice. There is a process of class-matching which goes on between student and university; a synchronisation of familial and institutional habitus.

Authenticity and social class

Rose (1998) writes about the dissemination of vocabularies for understanding and interpreting one's life and one's actions. In New Labour Britain with its emphasis on life long learning and 'education, education, education', it is increasingly assumed we will all develop our own personalised educational projects; that one major form of improvement and self-betterment comes through choosing more education:

> Become whole, become what you want, become yourself: the individual is to become, as it were, an entrepreneur of itself, seeking to maximise its own powers, its own happiness, its own quality of life, through enhancing its autonomy and then instrumentalising its autonomous choices in the services of its life-style. (Rose, 1998, p158)

Rose is writing about psychotherapy, but in the new millennium education has become another means of maximising and fulfilling the self. The UK now has more adults between the ages of 24 to 65 in training and education than any other nation in the OECD (Woodward, 2000). But this project of the self signifies differently for the working classes than for middle class individuals. Working class students are trying to negotiate a difficult balance between investing in a new improved identity and holding on to a cohesive self that retains an anchor in what had gone before; between escape and 'holding on' (Lawler, 2000). Such difficulties are compounded by age and make the transition to higher education particularly difficult for mature students:

> Educating yourself out of your own class, but doing it at an age where assimilating into the educated class is not realistic, not even entirely desirable, means that you become, for ever, neither fish nor fowl. (Freeborn, 2000, p10)

As Debbie's quote below exemplifies, working class students confront complex issues when attempting the transition to higher education

> There is a sort of community feel about Roehampton. It just seemed more of a community sort of feeling as opposed to a larger sized university and being lost within it. And being the type of person I am I like the idea I am going to be part of a community. (Debbie, Scottish working class FE student)

Underlying feelings of hopeful anticipation there are confusions and ambiguities about the sort of self they are seeking which the middle class students do not have to deal with to anything like the same extent. We glimpse shadows, hear whispers of what Bourdieu refers to as the most unexpected of all the dramas and conflicts that emanate from upward mobility: 'the feelings of being torn that come from experiencing success as failure, or, better still, as transgression' (Bourdieu, 1999, p510). Julie Bettie (2003) found a certain amount of ambivalence towards mobility in her study of white and Mexican American working class girls and this is echoed in our sample. The transcripts of the working class students hint at a delicate balance between realising potential and maintaining a sense of an authentic self. Amongst its many promises and possibilities, higher education also poses a threat to both authenticity and a coherent sense of selfhood for some working class students. Feelings of being an impostor are never far away. Education was, in the main, a world into which they fitted uneasily:

> I don't see the point in spending my time with people who are not going to be able to relate to me and I'm not going to be able to relate to them. We are from different worlds, so I think I've had enough of that in my life ... I don't want to feel as if I have to pretend to be someone I'm not. (Janice, Black working class lone parent)

We need then to set prevailing discourses of individualisation (Beck, 1992) against the more localised discourses of the mature working class students to see that Rose's project of becoming yourself is even more complicated for these students. Discourses of individualisation work to position the uncredentialled as unfinished, as incomplete in some way, while the cult of individualism can rapidly collapse into individual pathology (Ball *et al*, 2000). A significant number of the working class students had been variously confronting and avoiding dilemmas of educational failure throughout their educational careers. This shadow of earlier academic failure hung over the students' decision making. As Janice asserts 'I don't want to compete with anybody. I don't want to be in any of this competitiveness'. Such predispositions make the transition to higher education particularly difficult. But we would argue that for many of the working class students there is an additional dilemma around authenticity, which cuts across and confounds those arising from a sense of educational failure.

As we explore later in relation to Lesley and Angela's narratives, authenticity is a classed concept (Lawler, 2000). For the working class students authenticity most often meant being able to hold onto a self rooted in a working class past. In contrast, within prevailing discourses the authentic self, in Rose's (1998) terms 'the self seeking to maximise its own powers', is a self seeking to escape the fetters of working class existence. Such contemporary political and academic discourses increasingly represent working class existence as in the past, when traditional affiliations were intact, preventing self-realisation. As Beck puts, it 'status-influenced, class, cultural or familial biographical rhythms overlap with or are replaced by structural biographical patterns' (Beck, 1992, p131).

But Beck overstates the irrelevance of traditional affiliations – class remains, for these students, a crucial element of their identity, their sense of self. If university is too different, too alien, then the threat of losing oneself, as Debbie's words exemplify, is as likely a prospect as finding oneself. The struggle to find oneself implies finding somewhere where one can have a sense of belonging, however tenuous. This is especially problematic for the working class students, who have to negotiate tensions between maintaining a sense of authenticity in part rooted in social class and the desire to fit in. Perhaps this is another reason, over and above the powerful impact of material constraints (Reay et al, 2002), that working class students often prioritise the local and the familiar. It has become fashionable to dismiss any notion of working class communities as fantasised or illusory, yet such fantasies had real efficacy in the choice making of some of these working class students. Debbie's earlier evocation of community may have an unfashionable ring, but there are still traces in the working class students' narratives, and particularly in those of the mature students and the Bangladeshi students, of 'the localised milieu of collective experience out of which develop bounded lifestyles and political solidarities', that Thompson (1968, p109) described over thirty years ago. Referring to the area surrounding the college she wants to go to, Carole, a white working class mature student explains:

> I am really familiar with it over there. I just felt really comfortable thinking I was going over there in an area that I was familiar with, that I knew really well... That's one of the reasons I chose East London, not that I think there aren't going to be posh people there but just because I know I feel more comfortable there because I come from that area and I feel more centred, more rooted there.

Some of the middle class school students did talk about moving to cities or towns where they had family connections but none used the type of language evoked by working class students like Carole and Debbie. Most of these working class students were prioritising the safe and the familiar in the sense of attempting to find somewhere they might have a sense of belonging.

Cook (2000) writes about how judgments of taste are always imbricated in class. Educational choices are also never innocent of class when choosing either safety or risk. We make the educational choices we do, not despite class but because they express our classed differences from others. The exercise of educational choice is constantly aligning and realigning the boundaries between and within classes (Reay and Ball, 1997; 1998).

Intra-class differences: balancing risk and safety

These students, then, unlike their middle class counterparts, were making not one but sometimes two transitions in the move into higher education. Not only were they moving from one stage of education to another, a majority were also engaged in a transition from one class into another – a process that we have argued elsewhere (Reay et al, 2001) makes the higher education process qualitatively different to that being engaged in by the already middle class students. We can see glimpses of this qualitative difference in Sally's words:

> It's something that if I don't achieve this then I really don't see where I go from here. You know I've decided this is my next move. I've got to go on, I can't go back now, that's how I feel.

Particularly poignant is her entreaty 'I can't go back', suggesting a less desirable place she may be returned to if she fails to achieve. The same sense of falling back is not there in the middle class students' narratives.

Beck argues that 'one has to choose and change one's identity, as well as taking the risks in doing so' (Beck, 1992, p88). The difference between those who take and those who refuse such risks may rest upon differences between individualist and solidarist fractions of the working classes (Ball, et al, 2002). As more and more groups get caught up in the race for educational credentials, new internal class differentiations are emerging (Beck and Beck-Gernsheim, 2002). We want to explore dispositions for individualistic or more communal approaches to society as one possible source of working class internal differentiation, that cannot be explained simply by predicted academic attainment[1]. There was such a division in the sample between those working class students, predominantly mature students at FFEC, the Bangladeshi students at CCS, plus a small number of Scottish and Irish working class students (in all 24 out of the total 41), who demonstrated solidarist approaches to community and class, and some others who seemed to express a more individualistic approach. These latter students provide us with a different perspective on working class transitions to higher education than their more wary, working class counterparts. They chose all or mostly elite universities on their UCAS applications. Lesley, for example, defines herself as working class and is the first in her family to consider higher education. Yet at the same time, she clearly inhabits a class hinterland. Her father was self-employed and so is her partner. Lesley presents an interesting case of transition, as her negotiation of the higher education choice process exemplifies not only the tensions between security and challenge embedded in many of the narratives, but she also maps out a move from one end of the risk/risk aversion spectrum to the other:

> Originally I was only going to apply to Westminster because I really liked the sound of it and because I was doing it for me rather than vocational reasons, at the time that I was doing my UCAS form I thought I wanted to go somewhere that I was going to enjoy.

While initially Lesley expresses the same desire as many of the other students to go somewhere where she will feel happy and fit in, later, on the advice of a friend who is a lecturer, she changes her mind about the type of institution she wants to apply to. This shift could be attributed to many factors. Clearly her friend's advice had a significant effect, an interaction and the work of social capital which is more typical of our middle class respondents, but perhaps the greatest impact was her success on the access course which, she said, gave her 'an enormous confidence boost'. She was, perhaps more than all the other mature students apart from Penny, able successfully to redefine herself as academic.

Once Lesley has shifted her choice position she talks dismissively about the new universities, claiming that institutions like Middlesex either promote 'their great facilities' or else 'the opportunities for finding yourself'. While many of the other working class mature students were specifically prioritising the potential to find themselves, this is what Lesley wishes to avoid. She no longer wants to find herself in university but rather is seeking another better, improved academic self, that is to construct herself differently. Far from desiring to find herself she explicitly states that she 'doesn't want to be a member of any club that will have me'. She is engaged in a process of disaffiliation (Castells, 1997). Castells describes a process in which individuals disaffiliate from identities to which they are marginally attached and enter a world of fluidity and change where they can create a new self unconnected with their former social selves in school and in the family. Unlike a majority of the working class students, who are struggling to hold on to working class identities, Lesley is striving to leave her working class self behind.

According to Paul Ricoeur (1981; 1990), the achievement of the authentic self is enabled by the conventions of narrative. Narrative configures an identity in which the individual becomes who s/he always was. In Lesley's narrative the true self can only be realised through academic achievement and the attainment of middle class status. Charles Taylor (1992) argues, echoing aspects of Beck's thesis, that in contemporary society individuals feel compelled to realise their potential in order to achieve the true self; that they feel their lives would be somehow wasted or unfulfilled if they did not. Lesley fits Taylor's modern day version of the authentic self. She suggests that before, when she was considering Westminster, she was failing to prioritise academic aspects of choice; that it is no longer good enough to go somewhere where happiness and fitting in are the main criteria. However, her distinctions suggest oppositional understandings, almost as if she is working with an implicit either/or, in which the academic jostles uneasily with desires for happiness, fitting in and finding yourself. Despite 'desperately wanting to go to the London School of Economics', she still expresses anxieties about going to a place which she sees as 'very, very ambitious, ruthless even'.

The impossibility of a conjunction between academic success and finding yourself suggested in Lesley's text raises issues around what the academic signifies for these predominantly working class students. Authenticity is configured very differently for the twenty-four of the working class students who, we suggest, espouse solidarist working class dispositions. These twenty-four comprise a curious mixture of mature students from Black and white British traditional working class backgrounds, second generation Bangladeshi immigrants, and a small number of girls from Scottish and Irish manual working class backgrounds. These students seem to operate with a different conception of authenticity. Even for the young students with normative educational trajectories there is no easy union of the academic with personal satisfaction and achievement in their narratives. Any attempt at transformation runs all the risks of the academic failure and shame many experienced in their early schooling. As Janice says, 'I don't ever want that sick feeling in my stomach again'. Instead, most opt for safety and comfort: a combination of achieving educationally and still being able to be themselves in a way that stops short of transformation. As David asserts, 'my initial most important thing is that I'm comfortable. It is pretty much the most important thing for me'. On the basis of this criterion he turns down the offer of a place at King's, a college within the University of London, and opts to go instead to Roehampton, a new university and consequently far less prestigious.

David's authentic self does not have to be divested of its working classness. Rather, authenticity entails 'a special relationship with one's individual past and historical heritage' (Heidegger, 1962, p114). Far from overcoming one's past self, individuals must accommodate their past in order to have an authentic self. 'Authenticity is the loyalty of one's self to its own past, heritage and ethos' (Heidegger, 1962, p117). Unlike the middle class mature students in James' (1995) study, who were reshaping their identities in ways they know will put them closer to the people around them, the majority of the working class students were struggling to avoid identity shifts that would open up a distance between themselves and the working class communities they saw themselves as part of. Rather, in a similar process to the respondents in Archer *et al*'s (2003) study, they were engaged in difficult negotiations around identity in which the potential benefits in terms of improved opportunities, improved self, needed to be balanced against the potential costs of losing one's working class cultural identity, and with it a sense of authenticity.

Emotions in the choice process

Rational choice theory (Breen and Goldthorpe, 1997; Goldthorpe, 1998) banishes emotions from decision making, filling the space of choice with rational calculation and strategic choice. Yet the students' narratives, particularly those of the working class students, are full of emotion:

> Yes, it's been really really difficult. It ended up being really stressful because I was doing it in such a void. It's been really scary thinking that you could have made the wrong decision, very anxiety inducing ... I think it's more difficult if no one in your family's been there. I think in a funny sort of way it's more difficult if you're black too ... Because you want to go to a good university but you don't want to stick out like a sore thumb. It's a bit sad isn't it. I've sort of avoided all the universities with lots of Black students because they're all the universities which aren't seen as so good. If you're Black and not very middle class and want to do well then you end up choosing places where people like you don't go and I think that's difficult. (Candice, Black working class student, predicted two As and a B at A level)

We are not suggesting that working class students have more emotions than their middle class counterparts. Rather, there is a class difference in how emotions are expressed. The middle class students were often more tempered in their expression of emotions and we would argue that this is because there was less at risk for them in the choice process. Their resources of cultural, social and economic capital helped to alleviate feelings of risk, fear, shame and guilt (Reay, 2005). In contrast, the working class students, facing a strange and unfamiliar field, were often plagued with anxieties. In the quote above, Candice displays 'the anxiety about the future characteristic of students who have come from the social strata that are furthest away from academic culture and who are condemned to experience that culture as unreal' (Bourdieu and Passeron, 1979, p53). Shaun also found the whole process 'scary':

> It is very very worrying because I haven't got any safety nets any more. I really don't know what I'm going to do if the worst happens, if I don't get the grades for university. I am really really scared. It really is scary. (Shaun, Irish working class CCS, predicted two As and a C)

All the students were dealing with the pressures of having to get good enough grades and, to different degrees, were attempting to grapple with 'risky opportunities' (Beck, 1992). However, only the working class students used such powerfully emotive language of fear and anxiety. Young people from established middle class backgrounds, where there is a history of university attendance, far more often have a coherent story to tell about university choice, one with an easily discernable plot and a clearly defined beginning and end, despite episodic uncertainty and stressful periods. The discourses they draw on are those of entitlement and self-realisation. There is no lurking guilt or shame. There are also often extensive familial reserves of expertise and support to call upon. Unlike in Shaun's case, if the worst happens there are safety nets. No one talked of 'being scared' or 'in the dark':

> There's a family tug company in South America, which is a sort of relation on my mother's side, which, they pay my school fees, so it might be tactful to go and do a bit of work with them, and I might find it very interesting, and they employ family, so it is always a fall back if I am desperately unemployed in three years time. (George, white middle class CB)

The 'void' Candice talks about is filled for middle class students with relevant cultural, academic and social capital. Nick is reading the same subject at university as his father did. His interest in music began in primary school and has been a constant throughout his education:

> I have kind of grown up with the idea that going to university is just what people do. Basically, my dad did music at university, as well, so I had always been encouraged to do music, when I started learning instruments, which was six or seven, and although, at some stage I always wanted to give them up, but I kept them up, because I was encouraged, I wasn't forced to, by my parents. And that sort of formed the basis and I really got a passion for music. And that sort of passion is really the reason why I wanted to study at university, to find out more, and more so than any other subject,

so it was quite easy to decide, I knew well before I had to apply that I wanted to do music. So it was very easy. (Nick, white English middle class, CB)

The students from established middle class backgrounds, and particularly those at the two private schools, have stories to tell about the gradual, continual shaping of specific academic dispositions in which higher education choice is the logical end product of a host of earlier academic choices. In their texts choice is presented as rational, orderly, clear-cut, almost beyond question, very unlike the chancy, uncertain process Candice and Shaun are caught up in.

Working class fears and anxieties about the move into higher education are interwoven with desires to fit in and feel at home. Here we can see just how alien the class culture of the old universities can be for working class students both young and mature:

I was put off Goldsmiths', the interview there was really, really stressful. Oh, it was so stressful, it was two men and we'd done mock interviews here but it wasn't like that, this was kind of like what I'd imagined to be a conversation round a dinner table in a really upper class, middle class family and I was like 'Oh my God, I'm not ready for this. This is not for me'. It was awful. It was like they wanted me to have really strong views about things and I'm more maybe this maybe that. But they wanted someone who knew for certain what their feelings were but I kind of found myself thinking should I say this or should I say that? It was terrifying. (Maggie, white English working class FE student)

Working class students, particularly those like Candice, Maggie and Shaun who are aiming for elite universities, are having to juggle a welter of negative emotions alongside the positive feelings of excitement, pride and hopeful anticipation they share with middle class students. There is no need to emphasise the class nature of these anxieties because Candice articulates this clearly: 'I think it's more difficult if no one in your family has been there'. She also asserts that 'In a funny sort of way it's more difficult if you're Black too', illustrating the ways in which class and ethnicity are interwoven in the higher education choice process, and how their effects can amplify and deepen anxiety and fear.

Emotional capital (Reay, 2000; 2005) and its lack is also at issue here, with family emotional assets of confidence, security and entitlement in relation to the field of higher education all playing a part. Middle class emotional resources, particularly those of established middle class families (Allatt, 1993; 1996), alleviate stress and anxiety. In contrast, working class students felt a great deal of stress and anxiety when encountering the unfamiliar field of higher education. However, beyond fear and anxiety there is another emotion that compounds working class disadvantage. Shame and the fear of shame haunts working class relationships to education (Reay, 1997; Plummer, 2000). The conundrum for many of the working class students was that they were caught between two opposing shames. Firstly there was the shame of over-reaching and failing. This sense of failure was not simply academic. It implicated the individual far more holistically, in that a number of them seemed to feel that they failed to be the right person for traditional universities even when their level of achievement qualified them to apply. But if the first shame did not engulf, a second shame, evident in the narratives of Lesley and Angela, threatens:

> At the end of the day you want to say you've been to university and be proud of it, when people put their little university in brackets it's like that's where I did it. Not do it in really messy joined up writing so they can't understand it because you're ashamed of where you went to. (Angela, Irish working class FE student)

For a significant number of the working class students there were also glimmers of pride and a related desire to maintain class connections; an ethic of we, in contrast to an individualised I, which challenged contemporary notions of authenticity and provided for a more complex analysis of why these students sought out places where there were people like themselves. As Taylor argues;

> What we ought to be doing is fighting over the meaning of authenticity... we ought to be trying to persuade people that self-fulfillment, far from excluding unconditional relationships and moral demands beyond the self, actually requires these in some form. (Taylor, 1992, p72-3)

Throughout the students' accounts we catch glimpses of the working classes as the other of higher education. This positioning as other causes tensions for the working class students, tensions which raise powerful issues around authenticity, shame and belonging. This sense of being other can be further illuminated through Birgit's narrative. Birgit, half German, half English, from a family where no one has ever got beyond A levels or their German equivalent, is a mature student in her early thirties. She tells a story of applying to a number of universities, including Middlesex and SOAS, twice before. She first visited Middlesex in 1997 before she had signed up for the access course. Then she didn't like it because 'it was a bit posh, kind of upper class. Everything felt so separate, everybody felt separate. OK, we didn't know each other, but everything was so individual and I didn't get any vibes, nothing from the lecturers either. It was so sort of ... distant. Everybody seemed a bit stuffy and unfriendly'.

This account may sound implausible to academic insiders, aware that Middlesex as a new university is far less 'posh' than many other more established institutions. Yet they are not viewing the field of higher education from Birgit's vantage point. From where Birgit was positioned within the field of education in 1997, every higher education institution felt strange and distant. Like Archer and Hutchings' (2001) non-participant respondents, Birgit positions herself as outside of higher education, placing herself as potentially able to take advantage of the benefits it can offer but not as an owner of it.

In 2000 after four years of acculturation in FE, she applied again to SOAS and her very strong sense of feeling 'at a distance' has receded:

> Maybe it's me, maybe I've grown a bit more and come a bit further compared to the first time I went. Maybe that's got something to do with it. That I'm looking for different things not just an interesting course but a sense that the people there gel ... that I can get on with them. Because the first time I visited both Middlesex and SOAS I felt this distance.

Now, though, she feels 'more comfortable, more at ease of actually approaching people, so it is probably down to me, feeling more comfortable in myself'. Class acclimatisation clearly takes time and appears to operate in one direction only. The plot in Birgit's narrative hinges around her own transformation and draws heavily on individualised explanations of deficit and self improvement – namely that she has worked on herself and is now able to adapt more effectively to higher education culture.

An alternative account would stress a more collective explanation in which the cultural difference Birgit brought with her when she originally applied in 1997 represented a difference too far. In this version the distance which Birgit found so troubling is not a consequence of her failings but of hidebound institutions which do not know how to deal with difference, and especially class difference. Her subsequent acculturation through FE courses and two years of access, however, has made her more acceptable, less the other. In the first version Birgit's difference is the problem, whereas in the second version it is higher education's inability to deal with difference that is problematic.

Concluding comments

Within the working classes there are different class fractions with differing priorities in relation to risk, challenge and fitting in. These solidarist and individualist fractions within the working classes result in differing priorities, attitudes and actions in relation to the higher education choice process. Indeed working class individuals opting for higher education, even as mature students, could arguably be described as constituting a specific fraction within the working classes. They are already atypical. However, within this specific fraction we can see further differentiation between the majority who prioritise risk aversion, fitting in and feeling comfortable and a minority, like Lesley, who give primacy to challenge and risk. Although existing research recognises different fractions within the middle classes (Butler, 1997; Butler and Savage, 1995; Savage et al, 2001; Power et al, 2003; Ball, 2003), there is far less work on diversity and heterogeneity within the working classes. However, this research highlights the importance of identifying and working with intra-working class differences. Very different imagined futures are not only being envisaged but acted out in the choice process within as well as across social class. In particular, belonging to individualist or solidarist fractions within the working classes generates different priorities, attitudes and actions in relation to higher education access and choice.

This chapter also problematises the concept of widening participation within contemporary discourses, indicating that despite the superficial noisy welter of innovation, at a deeper more impenetrable level certain structures of privilege remain impervious to change (Burke, 2002). These prevailing inequalities make the transition to higher education particularly difficult for mature working class students like Birgit who must fashion themselves in the image of the traditional higher education applicant, risking inauthenticity, or else restrict themselves to those universities, in a minority within the pre-1992 sector, with mature student friendly policies. It is this difficulty in dealing with class difference, particularly among the pre-1992 sector of higher education that the widening participation initiatives will need to address.

Widening participation is intended to open up higher education to working class students. Yet class inequalities of access to universities endure, despite the many widening participation initiatives designed to attract working class students (Wakeford, 1993; Burke, 2002). In particular, the proportion of mature students in higher education fell during the late 1990s from 22 per cent in 1994 to 18 per cent in 2000 and only regained its 1994 level in 2003 (Abrams, 2003).

So are policy commitments to widening participation reality or empty rhetoric? Certainly there is a powerful contradiction between the Government's expressed commitment to widening participation and recent funding changes which have severe exclusionary repercussions for working class students. We would also stress the importance of setting the rhetoric of widening access and opportunities for working class students within a context of constraints – material, practical and psychological. Widening participation in this sense is both under-theorised and under-researched. In reference to Lareau and Weininger's (2003) definition of cultural capital quoted in chapter 2, it is clear that many of our working class students lack the necessary capitals to cope and respond successfully to the demands inherent in the transition to higher education. No wonder there are such high drop out rates in new universities with large working class intakes.

Where does this leave widening participation as an initiative? The stories working class students tell demonstrate determination, commitment, adaptability and many more triumphs of the will. There is much to celebrate. Yet, as we have also glimpsed from these students' narratives, widening participation has to date been all about grand designs and inadequate realisations. Opportunities have to be set against constraints. Government rhetoric lauds and celebrates the former, but our data highlights the power and continuing influence of the latter. At the same time, emphasising structure is not the same as arguing that there is uniformity of class conditions, practices and outcomes. As this chapter has demonstrated, class is always mediated by ethnicity, age and gender, and these mediations are played out in the working class students' negotiations of the higher education process. In the next chapter we focus on the mediations of ethnicity by examining the choice processes of the ethnic minority students in our sample.

Note

1 Although more of the individualist working class grouping were predicted high exam results so were a number of the solidarist group.

6

Culture, community and choice: ethnic minority students

There is a substantial body of research on the issue of ethnic minority access to higher education. But much less work has been done on ethnic minority students' experiences of higher education and almost none on how such students choose the higher education institution they attend. In this chapter we concentrate on the 65 ethnic minority students in our sample. First, we focus on how the processes, concerns, resources and outcomes of choosing differ among the ethnic minority students in relation to social class. Class differences are more apparent and significant than ethnic or cultural similarities. Second, we discuss the importance of ethnic mix. For a large minority of these students, 25 of the 65, the ethnic mix of higher education institutions is one factor, among others, that influences their choice. Ethnic mix is examined and discussed in relation to ethnic identity.

There is a solid body of literature which addresses the issue of patterns of higher education access for ethnic minority students (e.g. Taylor, 1992, Modood and Shiner, 1994, Abbasi, 1998, Modood and Acland, 1998; Connor *et al*, 2004)) and a small amount of work on minority students' experience of higher education (e.g. Bird, 1996, Osler, 1999) but almost nothing has been written on how ethnic minority students choose among HEIs.

This chapter is based upon a close analysis of interviews with 65 ethnic minority (minority)[1] students including 16 Jewish students: 35 women and 30 men, from the total of 120 interviewed in the study. The backgrounds, identities and class positions of the minority students are diverse – see Table 7.

Two things need to be made clear. First, ethnic minority choice of higher education is situated within a variety of other criteria, constraints, concerns and possibilities of choice, many of which are articulated or experienced by any student. Ethnicity on its own does not explain or account for the choices of ethnic minority students. Second and concomitantly, any generalisations about the minority students in our sample are misleading. Differences among the minority students in terms of social class and educational inheritance are clearly important and these differences are played out in applications and admissions to higher education. This is one of the main themes of this chapter. As Modood and Shiner (1994 p4) warn: 'It is ... not appropriate to speak of a white-ethnic minority divide'.

Table 7 Ethnicity and Gender of the minority sub-sample

Ethnicity	male	female	Total
Bangladeshi	4	3	7
Sri Lankan	1	1	2
Indian	5		5
Pakistani		1	1
African Caribbean		1	1
Nigerian	2	3	5
Ghanan		1	1
Ugandan		1	1
Philipino		1	1
Chinese	3	1	4
Jordanian	1		1
Algerian	1		1
Iranian	2	1	3
Guyanese		1	1
Black British	4	4	8
Mixed-race	2	5	7
Jewish	5	11	16
Total	**30**	**35**	**65**

Ethnic minority, as we shall see, is a very diverse analytic category. In some respects therefore this provides a vehicle for discussion of some general and generic issues about choice but it is also the case that there are some aspects of choice that are specific to or particularly bear upon ethnic minority students. That is, the nature of or criteria for choice combine in particular ways for some minority students. In relation to our research as a whole then this chapter attempts to put ethnicity in context. In the table above and the extracts quoted below, with two exceptions, the ethnicities attributed to the students are those used by the students themselves.

The London setting for the research is, as we shall see, important in the concerns, experiences and perceptions of the students. They view the world of higher education from a London perspective and this is particularly important in relation to issues related to the ethnic mix of higher education institutions. Forty four per cent of Britain's minority population live in Greater London compared with 10 per cent of England's total white population (CRE, 1999) and that 20 per cent of the London population are identified by the ONS (2001) as members of minority groups; 22 per cent of the population of London were born outside of the UK. The distribution of these groups within London is very uneven. For example, in 2001 27 per cent of the population of Camden and 54 per cent of Brent were ethnic minorities compared with less than 9 per cent in Richmond. Furthermore, 40 per cent of all ethnic minority higher education students are in London HEIs, mainly in the new universities.

We want to begin by constructing two contrasting ideal types of minority chooser. In the spirit of the disclaimers above, many facets of the types are evident across our sample as a whole[2]. The ideal types work as a set of simple binaries and have all the drawbacks of such a formulation but here they are intended to set up a base line or framework for further, more nuanced discussion later in the chapter. They should not be mistaken for descriptive categories. They are, in Weber's terms, hypothetical selections, a step away from reality. A few students do fit fairly neatly into one or the other but that is not the point or purpose here.[3]

For want of better terms or markers the two types are referred to as *contingent* and *embedded* choosers. These may also be thought of as two different discourses of choice. The social conditions of choice for each type are different. Some of the major differences are summarised in Table 8. Note, however, that this is not a stark and total antithesis – after all the students reported here are all wanting/intending to go on to higher education, with varying degrees of enthusiasm. The similarities between them must be borne in mind as well as the differences.

Table 8. Ideal types of HE Chooser

Contingent choosers	Embedded choosers
finance is a key concern and constraint	finance is not an issue
choice uses minimal information	choice is based on extensive and diverse sources of information
choice is distant or 'unreal'	choice is part of a cultural script, a 'normal biography'
few variables are called up	a diverse array of variables are deployed
choice is general/abstract	choice is specialist/detailed
minimal support (social capital) is used	extensive support (social capital) is mobilised
ethnic mix is an active variable in choosing	ethnic mix is marginal or irrelevant to choice
choosing is short term and weakly linked to 'imagined futures' – part of an incomplete or incoherent narrative	choosing is long term and often relates to vivid and extensive 'imagined futures' – part of a coherent and planned narrative
first-time' choosers with no family tradition of HE	followers embedded in a deep grammar of aspiration which makes HE normal and necessary
narrowly defined socioscapes and spatial horizons – choices are local/ distance is a friction	broad socioscapes and social horizons – choices are national/ distance is not an issue
parents as onlookers or weak framers/mothers may give practical support'	parents as strong framers and active participants in choice

It is important to explain and illustrate these differences. In each case data from a small number of students are deployed to illustrate the types. The illustrations are used to indicate the complexity of choosing in the interrelationships among the characteristics of the types. These illustrations stand for the patterns identified within the whole sub-sample. Later we begin to muddy some of these neat but crude distinctions and further data are referred to.

The contingent chooser

The contingent chooser is typically a first generation applicant to higher education whose parents were educated outside of the UK. Their parents are working class and have low incomes. The student can expect little financial support from them in choice-making or funding higher education. Although there may well be emotional support and high levels of encouragement and expectation within the family for the achievement of credentials, any emotional support provided seldom operates as a resource that can mobilised productively in the choice making process. Mothers sometimes figure large in giving practical support and encouragement.[5] But expectations are generic and sometimes unrealistic and weakly linked to real imagined futures. Higher education becomes a break or hiatus in family and personal narratives. The decision to apply for higher education or the realisation of higher education as a possible next step is recent – made at the end of GCSEs or during A-level courses. Higher education and getting a degree are general categories; neither family nor student have much sense of the different kinds and statuses of higher educations on offer nor of what higher education study will be like: 'the new system with its fuzzy classifications and blurred edges encourages and entertains ... aspirations that are themselves blurred and fuzzy' (Bourdieu and Passeron, 1979, p91) and not surprisingly 'faulty perceptions ... are encouraged by the anarchic profusion of courses' (p92).

The status distinction between old and new universities is either not recognised or not seen as significant. The processes of information gathering and choice are mostly left to the student, who often will act on the basis of very limited information. Reliance on a few significant others for 'hot knowledge' is high – that is, first or second hand recommendations or warnings related to specific institutions based on some kind of direct experience (Ball and Vincent, 1998) – but contingent choosers end up relying more heavily on cold knowledge (mostly relying on prospectuses) than do their embedded counterparts. Their social capital is of limited relevance here. The student and family have fewer direct links to higher education experiences and in many instances none. At this point they are 'condemned to experience [the culture of higher education] as unreal' (Bourdieu and Passeron, 1979, p53). Subjects rather than courses are discussed and distinctions between institutions do not operate at the level of differences in course structures or content or teaching strategy. Visits to institutions or attendance at open days are rare[6]. Contingent choosers 'might be described as working on the surface structure of choice, because their programmes of perception rest upon a basic unfamiliarity with particular aspects' (Gewirtz, Ball and Bowe, 1995, p47) of higher education. Spatial horizons of action are limited; partly for reasons of cost and partly as a result of concerns about ethnic fit and ethnic mix and the possibility of confronting racism. Institutions which offer an ethnic mix, with good numbers of the students' own ethnicity but no predominant group, are favoured. Leaving London or leaving home is rarely an option for these students, although some would be keen to do so if circumstances allowed. Modood and Shiner, (1994, p38) note that a disproportionate number of minority students make applications to their home regions (as does Taylor, 1992). Family and community relationships are positively valued and local choices also reflect this. Staying at home may also be a factor which offsets the potential isolation reported by minority students in some HEIs (see Bird, 1996, Taylor, 1992, p369).

Let us look at some data to illustrate and fill out this general description. The vignettes presented below were chosen to illustrate variety within the types rather than simple commonality.

Jamaal came to the UK from Bangladesh when he was six. He has seven brothers and two sisters and his family are mainly involved in restaurant work. He attends CCS. He 'can't remember' his parents giving him any educational advice, 'I think they were more worried about my elder brothers getting jobs'. None of his family had stayed on at school to do A levels. When choosing his A levels he first had in mind a job in aeronautical engineering but then switched to medicine and chose physics, chemistry and maths. He explained: 'in my family you're seen to do really really well if your son becomes a doctor'. But he 'couldn't really handle' physics and dropped it in favour of sociology; 'it was one of my other friends ... he said it was really interesting'. Jamaal is now hoping to do social science at university. 'I haven't got any plans, I just want to get a degree and see what happens later on in social science, I'm really interested in international relations but I don't know'. His UCAS choices were Westminster, East London, Luton, Middlesex and London Metropolitan. He would have liked to have had the option to apply outside the London area but practical constraints made this impossible. There were four main factors underlying this selection:

> It was mainly, you know, where I can have contact with my relatives and so on ... It has to do with my family but also my friends. Also obviously I wanted to stay in London and obviously the predicted grades were also a factor. And also the financial aspect ... but I wanted to go outside London if I could.

Jamaal admitted that he knew 'not much' about the places he had chosen – 'I just looked up the prospectuses and that's about it'. But he does have 'a lot of friends who are in different universities'. The points offers made by the different institutions are a prime consideration in Jamaal's thinking but this is weighed against other factors – like the possibility of encountering racism and his preference for an institution with a high proportion of Asian and Muslim students:

> Luton asked me for 16 points too but the thing is with Luton, it is a very racist area, so that has put me off. Now I know I don't really want to go there ... There's been recent headlines in the news and also my friends there have experienced racism. One of my friends transferred from Luton to Sussex [and] Asian families are generally close-knit, so they stick together so I'd want to go somewhere where there were other Asian students ... Most of the universities that I have chosen have Islamic Societies, I mean that would be an indicator that they don't discriminate and stuff.

Cassie is dual heritage. Her mother is a mature entrant to teaching and her father a social worker; both are graduates of the University of North London. Her parents are separated and she lives with her mother. She is doing GNVQ courses at MU and wants to do a degree in business management with 'the idea of getting into hotel work. I would like to manage a hotel'. This came from 'my aunt, she worked as a maid in a hotel, and she used to tell the stories about famous people and stuff ... and I like to travel ... and you get to meet a lot of new people'. It was 'mum' who suggested business management. 'We were talking about it and she said it might be best' but 'she didn't mind, she said if that was what I wanted to do then that was alright'. Cassie wants to go to higher education outside London 'but not too far' and 'got the UCAS book and rung up loads of universities and looked at the entry requirements and stuff'. She also looked on the UCAS website but has not visited any of her choices. Her mum is 'looking forward to me moving out ... but she said I could stay if I want to'.

She applied to Chester, Suffolk, Southampton and London Metropolitan. She had put down Oxford Brookes but they changed their GNVQ requirement to a distinction and so 'I couldn't go there any more'. She 'had heard from my uncle's partner that it was a good university'. Her first choice is now Chester: 'They've got a good night life there and the university looks really nice' and 'I would prefer to be right in the city centre rather than tucked up in some village in the middle of nowhere'. She believes that it is only two and a half hours from London. Her mum and dad will both help with costs and ' I hope to find a part time job'. Cassie wants a 'place of my own, my own space... and experience what life is like'. Her mother does not mind where she goes 'as long as I go to university I suppose'. Cassie's friend Carrie has also chosen Chester and that was a key factor – they wanted to be together but 'We did talk about it being white [laughs]'. Mum and Dad said:

> I should got to an area that is like mixed. And has got like a whole kind of different, lots of people of all different races... and that if you're mixed race that's the best thing to do ... Carrie wanted to go to Wales and that was not a place for me ... there's quite a lot of mainly white people there, so I thought it would be quite boring...

Cassie found choosing and making her application stressful and relied on 'mum mainly ... It was very hard'.

Adeibe's parents are from Algeria. His father is a radio engineer and his mother a nursery worker. He attends the MU consortium.

When he was young he wanted to work on television and 'be famous' but he had 'never' talked to his parents about what he might do when he finished school. Careers advisers had suggested computer design but he 'wanted to do something with science' and his family (despite his 'never') 'said that would be best for me'. He chose A-level Biology, Design Technology and Maths. When confronted with a UCAS application Adeibe had to decide what he wanted to do. His family 'helped me pick a university' and 'my mum phoned up for me to different universities'. He did not visit any universities or attend the Higher Education Fair but he did make some phone calls and used the UCAS web-site. He did not find school 'helpful really ... they didn't give me any ideas where I should apply'. He did not discuss his choice with teachers or friends but 'my mum helped me a lot'. He had no other advice: 'I don't really know anyone who has been to uni apart from a friend of my dad ... I wanted to do something in science with sports ... I just went through and picked the ones that I liked' from a list of 'about thirty' within his 18 point target range. Mum 'wanted me to do what I thought best [but] she helped me finalise universities'.

Adeibe wanted 'somewhere in a big city' but not 'too far' and 'easy to get to' and 'cheaper' than London, and the social life 'was one of my main things' although his mother did not think this important. He selected Bristol, Nottingham, UCL, Hertfordshire and Greenwich. He 'wasn't bothered about league tables', though he did look at them, or about old and new universities. Neither did he look at social or ethnic mix; he 'didn't know about that'. Nottingham is his first choice. He has been to the city a couple of times: 'It has a nice feel about it'. His dad will 'set up a fund' to help pay for university but 'I will have to work' and take out a loan. He has not thought about what jobs he might do after university.

Shamina is Bangladeshi. She has a brother who is an accountant and went to Westminster University. She started thinking about A levels while at Saturday school and discussed it with her family. She attends CCS. She chose A level Media Studies and Sociology and is predicted two Cs at A level. Her parents were 'really happy' that she decided to stay on and said that 'you have to basically do A levels and go on to a degree if you want the chance of a good job ... I was born in this country and went through the whole education system here, so because of that they want me to go to further education and study at University'. Shamina was unsure of what course to apply for and 'was confused about what to do'. She thought about social policy and 'read up a bit about that'. Her 'sister-in-law does social policy and management at London Metropolitan ... and she was telling me it's really good stuff' but 'I want to do something else, something to do with crime and law ... so then I came up with criminology'.

Guided by her teacher, Shamina decided on criminology and social policy combined. But as for university, again 'she was confused', like her friends: 'we were all finding it too hard to choose'. Prospectuses 'didn't tell you everything you needed to know' but she also looked at some University websites. Eventually 'I was in a rush and panicking' and 'I put Kingston, Middlesex, South Bank, Westminster, East London and Thames Valley, all London basically because I wanted to study in London ... I didn't want to go outside London. It's quiet to me, not busy, I don't like it'. But this is also to do with finances 'because living at home would be much cheaper ... because you don't need to pay for the rent and food'. She also looked at UCL but 'they wanted too many points'. Middlesex is Shamina's first choice, although she has not been there and her knowledge of the university is rather thin; 'my friend went there already and said it's a really nice place, they have all the facilities there to do with her course'.

Clearly, 'hot knowledge' and personal recommendations are highly valued when available. Shamina's brother said Westminster was 'good, but at the end of the day it's up to me'. A friend is also going to Middlesex 'but if I have to go somewhere where there is no one I know I'd still go'. Travelling is not an issue, although Shamina is a little vague about where Kingston is 'but I think I can manage them all'. As to costs, her parents say 'we will help you as much as we can ... We will be beside you' but she will need to work part-time and take out a loan.

The priorities and position and also the unreality, of higher education for the contingent chooser are epitomised by Sheila, a Black British young women who lives independently in a hostel and is dependent upon welfare benefits. City University is her first choice. She was asked why.

> I don't even know anything about the University. I've read the
> prospectus and the way media and sociology are described it
> sounded really great and it's in the city and it will be beneficial
> economically, I think, because I spent so much money to get to
> college and it's nearer than Brunel. Brunel is miles out!

Contingent choosers know little about the institutions they choose,
even their first choice universities. Choosing is a process involving
the balance of practical constraints with a limited number of
positive criteria. These criteria are primarily extrinsic; all 'extra-
vagances' are excluded (Bourdieu, 1990b, p56). The frictions and
vagaries of distance impinge firmly upon choice. Despite the
cosmopolitan experiences of these young people and links with
family across the world, their actual 'socioscapes'', or 'real geo-
graphies of social action' (Harvey, 1989, p355), are relatively com-
pressed or foreshortened. They inhabit very different 'time-space
biographies' (Hagerstrand, 1975) from those of the embedded
choosers.

The embedded chooser

The embedded chooser has parents who attended university and
often other relatives and friends with experience of university,
although not necessarily in the UK. University attendance is a well-
established and expected route beyond school, part of a 'normal
biography' (Du Bois-Reymond, 1998). Such students are subject
to subtle and 'diffuse incitements' (Bourdieu and Passeron, 1979,
p20) to further study. Not to go on to higher education is virtually
unthinkable and certainly unacceptable to parents. Thus the
singularity of individual dispositions are positioned firmly 'within
the class and its trajectory' (Bourdieu, 1990b, p60). University is
often linked to particular career trajectories and entry into prestigious professions or highly-paid commercial occupations.

Career aspirations are often long standing and vividly imagined,
part of a coherent and connected personal narrative. They are
common-sensical and self-evident. The family are able to mobilise
various forms of support and information for the student, like
arranging work experience or discussions with people in target
occupations. Parents are directly involved in choice-making, for
instance in making visits to universities and commenting on UCAS
application forms. Types of information used in choice-making are

diverse and value is given to both 'hot' and 'cold' knowledge, league table positions being a significant example of the latter.

The nature of courses as well as institutions are attended to. Cost is not the pressing issue that it is for contingent choosers, and is either taken for granted or openly discussed and settled by parents. The type and status of University attended is important but location is a secondary issue. It is expected that if necessary the student will move out of the family home and away from London to get the right course and the right institution. Such students approach higher education choice with confidence and certainty. At this point they are in many respects akin to Bourdieu and Passeron's (1979, p53) 'bourgeois students, who make higher education an experience into which enter no problems more serious than those they put there'. Some of these choosers would prefer institutions that are ethnically mixed but do not expect to find a problem with racism in higher education settings. Some illustrations will put flesh onto this outline.

Sarah's parents come from Ghana and they both attended Manchester University. Her older brother is also at Manchester doing Materials Science. Her sister is reading Economics at Coventry. Her father is a lecturer in biochemistry and her mother a midwife. She attends CCS. 'My parents have always told us: you are all going to university ... so it has always been sort of automatic for me ... It's not like I had the choice'. But Sarah wants 'to go to university anyway and I've heard too much about how good it is'. From watching *LA Law*, Sarah decided she wanted to be a lawyer and 'my dad showed me a few things in the encyclopaedia and helped me find stuff about it'. She asked her Careers Advisers which would be the best universities for law. 'They said those with the best reputation were Cambridge, Oxford, Manchester, Bristol and Warwick but that every single university that teaches law is good' and 'they told me to look at the universities that have a lot of people getting jobs after they finished their degree...'.

Sarah became 'quite firm about the ones I wanted to go to' and, again, 'my dad had already told me alot of stuff'. She perused prospectuses, used the UCAS CD-rom and attended the Higher Education Fair and 'learned a lot about the universities in the way they presented themselves'. She also went with a school trip to the Manchester universities. She reacted quite differently to each. At Manchester 'the first thing they spoke about to us was education, they talked about the course ... showed us the libraries and stuff, it was really good'. Manchester Metropolitan 'was such a contrast' they were shown a video of 'the social life and we saw people drinking ... and then they took us to the gyms and that... It put me off'.

Sarah is predicted two Cs and a D at A level. 'So I thought to myself. I've no chance of Oxford or Cambridge, although those are the best places to go to, let's get real ... so I applied to Manchester Met ... Sussex, Leeds, Leeds Met, Cheltenham and Thames Valley'. She plans to visit Sussex and Swansea and 'ask my dad to come'. She has a conditional offer of three Bs from Sussex, her first choice. And she does not 'mind at all whether it's a city or not. It just depends where I can get in'. She is fed up with London and 'I wanted to get away, I wanted to be independent. I don't want my family around, you know ... [and] they would have preferred me to go away and experience being away from the family'.

Sarah's parents were helpful with the UCAS form: 'my dad found a few mistakes ... they were very helpful. they'd been through it with my brother and sister'. She did look at the league tables but says that they 'might tell you which ones are successful but it depends on what kind of person you are because I could go to a top university and absolutely hate it ... it didn't really affect my choice'. The ethnic makeup of the universities did interest Sarah:

> I did read about the African Caribbean societies and the Asian societies and all the different things they do, and I know there are quite a few people, a few black people and Asian people who do go to Sussex and Manchester Met and stuff like that and that was important that they had those sorts of societies there. It means you know you're not going to be the only black person there. So I know the population is predominately white in Sussex, but even then that didn't affect me really, because I thought as long as there are some black people there, and there are some Asian people there, and Chinese people there, whatever, I don't mind because I prefer to be somewhere where there is different cultures. And so I did make sure that there was a mix yes...

Sarah's parents will 'be able to help contribute' to the costs of higher education but 'there are so many things they could do with their money, more important than bailing me out'. Both her brother and sister worked their way through university 'and they seem quite all right' and 'I'll borrow the money. I'm determined to get a law degree. And if I'm in debt I'll pay it somehow'. She has discussed university with friends as well as family and has begun to develop a sense of some of the real demands and possibilities involved.

> Simon, my friend has gone to Imperial, and I've spoken to him a lot about stuff like that, my friend has gone to Liverpool University to do a medicine degree, she got two As and a B, so she knows a lot about that. My other friend went to Bristol, so I do have quite a few friends who have been to university, and some who started university a year ago. You know, in London, so I have spoken to them a lot about university.

Sarah explained that the course she took was more important to her than the university and she preferred 'the modern way of teaching things'.

Navid came to the UK from Iran when he was six. His father is a lawyer. One sister did accountancy at South Bank, the other is doing medicine at Manchester. He attends CB. Higher education has always been on the cards – 'it is just the culture I am from, it is expected. No one usually drops out, in Iran, where I am from, it is sort of expected of you. Not really expected, as in there's pressure put on you, but sort of something you don't think about – oh well, I'll drop it at sixteen, it's not really an option'. None of his family or family friends have failed to go to university. Here we see habitus as predisposition 'without any calculation' (Bourdieu, 1990b, p53) at work. '... your parents sort of expect you to do well, in a way, and so you have that responsibility, and you sort of just work towards it. And I always knew that I was going to be a scientist, so it wasn't a problem to me, I was looking forward to A levels actually ... the decision of my going into A levels wasn't a decision. It was what shall I study at A level'.

Navid developed high expectations for himself which reflected the culture of his private school. 'When we were looking at A levels and everything, loads of people were doing four A levels and going to Oxford and Cambridge, and I made myself a sort of promise that I would want to do four A levels, it doesn't matter what I did, I just wanted to put pressure on myself and see if I could cope. And to this day I have regretted that I didn't apply to Oxbridge'. But he wants to become a dentist and explained that 'King's and Bristol are the Oxbridge of Dentistry'. His choice of career was backed up with considerable research and embedded in an unusually vivid sense of what such work would and could entail.

> ... so many people I talk to go – oh, a dentist, that just 'means you have to look at people's mouths all day. But if you just take it a step beyond that, when you look at what it actually is, it is a stable job, it is connected with the sciences, and there is a wide variety of things you can get into. I was quite interested in medicine before, but then I sort of, the surgical side of medicine, the extreme, extensive surgery, I just do not find interesting. So I sort of, I looked at the career options I had and dentistry seemed ideal... they asked me at one of my interviews, what type of thing do you want to go post graduate in? And I said – well, definitely not maxi-filial surgery. And they said – why? And I said it was just something that just doesn't appeal to me. I prefer to be in contact with the patient and have a relationship with them, rather than to anaesthetise them and just perform surgery on them.

He saw this as an interesting and sensible decision. 'I had the opportunity to go off and do something which I also enjoy and which will get me some money and make a stable life for myself'. Navid's choice narrative offers a particularly coherent and highly organised account of his educational career in relation to his expectations of a future work career, the more so in that Navid embeds his decisions within an extensive social network. He discussed his choice with:

> Dr Anderson (Head of 6th form) especially, and Mr Rumsey, because he used to be a teacher and we are quite close ... I asked them a lot of questions, they guided me, but I think the most influential people were, I've got quite alot of dentist friends. People who have come from Sweden and people who have graduated here, and the person I did my work shadowing with ... in summer I usually go to Iran to visit all the family, and I worked with an orthodontist and that was quite revealing... my mum's cousin owns the clinic...

Navid also discussed higher education with his GP. 'He said don't not go to King's, it's too good an opportunity to miss'. His view of the high reputation of dentistry at King's was well researched. 'I know at least seven or eight people who have studied either medicine or dentistry at King's'. There is a considerable body of social capital in play here. And he was also secure in the notion that he would be comfortable at King's. 'I think there will be people who will suit my social interests...'. Like other private school students Navid displays the predispositions of a habitus 'pre-adapted to such a milieu' (Bourdieu, 1990b, p61) and 'a strategy without strategic design' (Bourdieu, 1990a, p108). There is a sense here of what Bourdieu (1990a, p108) calls 'ontological complicity'. In all this Navid's parents provided a strong frame of expectation; 'if I said I was going to drop out after A levels I think they would have something to say about that'. But he expected his parents to be hands-off in relation to choice: 'I don't think my dad has influenced any of us in our choices ... They shouldn't really interfere'. Navid had no interest in the presence of other Iranian students. Indeed he disavows any cultural commonality (see below): 'I am not culturally towards Iranian, actually I am quite the reverse'. But he did express a preference for a location with cultural mix: 'it sort of makes me feel better that I know people from different cultures'.

More that anything else the minority students in the private schools reflect the values, choices and concerns of their school peers. The private school students share identities, attitudes and actions. Minority students like Navid are able to deploy as a resource what could be termed transnational cultural capital, forms of legitimate knowledge that have efficacy within the field of UK higher education.

Lena is Black British with a South African mother with an art foundation qualification and a Ghanaian father with an engineering degree from Ghana. She attends the MU consortium. All her education has been in the UK and she described herself as 'totally academic'. She got nine A stars and an A at GCSE. Her career choice, for some time, had been between Law and Medicine, but she did work experience at the Law Centre 'and really hated that ... It was so boring ... just paperwork'. Her parents 'support me: they said – you can do whatever you want basically'. She did more work experience in GPs' surgeries and 'really liked that'. Her form teacher's brother, a doctor, helped organise the placements. In year 12 she 'was asked by some teachers if I wanted to apply for sort of

Oxbridge and I said no then'. The reasons were simple: 'I want to stay in London, , and at the time I liked Imperial and UCL. That's where I wanted to go'. She 'knows GPs who teach there, one at Imperial and one at UCL, and they both recommended'.

Again we see that Lena's choice has become vivid for her and is embedded in a stock of social capital on which she can draw for information, access, sponsorship and support. She does voluntary work in a local hospital one afternoon a week. Although she had decided against Oxbridge the school kept up 'lots of pressure' and 'so I applied to Cambridge as well'; although her mother was not keen: 'she said you know the debt I would be in by the end of it would be so high. That it would be financially much better to live at home'. One of Lena's teachers, whose daughter was reading medicine at Cambridge, arranged for the girls to meet. From this and her other contacts and work experience she acquired a good grasp of the different degree and training structures for Medicine and could compare the different courses in some detail.

Lena visited Oxford with two friends and a teacher who had been a student there, and then went with three friends to see Cambridge; 'we arranged to visit a few colleges'. The facility of all this contrasts with the laboured and distant choices of the contingent choosers. Lena applied to New Hall – 'it was impressive' – but she was 'underwhelmed' by Cambridge itself – 'it was just a little town'. As to the other students she was aware that 'they are sort of middle class' but 'didn't really mind that' although her two friends were 'put off' by 'the posh people who will look down on me'. Here we see the limits of 'ontological complicity' and the natural milieu of higher education made unnatural. Lena is made aware of the 'sense of one's place' and the 'sense of the place of others' (Bourdieu, 1990a, p113). She attended three interviews and took a test and 'thought it was brilliant' and says she was 'seduced by the ivory towers stuff'. She was not offered a place and was also turned down by the Royal Free and is now waiting to hear from UCL and Imperial. Her mum 'is pleased, she didn't want me to go'. The UCL interview day was full of familiar faces, 'rejects from Cambridge', but 'more talkative, a bit more friendly'. She is now less worried about costs: 'I've decided I'm just gonna go for it and take out loans ... And so I am going to stay at home and that will reduce it a bit, I've got a Sunday job, so that will help a little more'.

So far all our embedded choosers come from highly credentialled, established middle class families. However a few ethnic minority students who are more tenuously located as middle class, also display many of the characteristics of an embedded chooser, whilst revealing a degree of deliberation and improvisation more characteristic of contingent choosers. Wing is Chinese and attends RC. She was born in the UK, her parents come from Hong Kong, they own and run their own shop. None of her family 'has ever been to university'. Her interests are in Business Studies and economics and she is good at maths. She already has a sense of a future for herself linking the here and now to a foreseeable work life. 'I wanted to go into like the financial sector. When I've done a degree in economics... maybe after I get my degree, work for a company and go abroad for a bit, if I could go to America and come back and stuff'. She was not sure what university but 'I wanted to go to a good university ... depending how well I do in my A levels'. She is already 'hoping to do an extra year and get a Masters degree'.

Wing sought advice from the brother of a friend who 'went into economics and he's like got a job in it and everything. So he was really aware of which universities are quite well known for having good economic departments'. Wing checked in the subject league tables, 'not looking in the overall tables but the subject' and in addition, 'my economics teacher was telling me'. The careers office 'didn't really help me'. Again specialist, first hand advice is better than second hand and general advice. From Wing's knowledge gathering LSE and Bristol emerged, although Cambridge was top of the league table. Wing had two interviews with the RC Oxbridge advisers, but 'I don't think my grades would be good enough'. She also consulted *Which University?* which she found helpful because as well as the subject 'it's about the place, the city...'. The courses appeared 'quite similar'.

Wing has offers for five of her UCAS choices, 'all kind of quite high actually' but prefers LSE, her first choice. 'I think it's the best place and also I want to stay in London ... because I want to go into the financial sector and London is the main city'. She went to the LSE

Open Day and 'it's quite nice I liked it, it's very city like. It's not like a university as you imagine'. It is interesting that Wing had imagined what a university would be like. Leeds is her insurance place – 'a few of my friends have been up there and loved it'. She will go to the Open Day. All her choices are for city universities: 'I want to stay in a city... I didn't really fancy going to the country-side'. A part of this is to do with ethnic mix and a concern about racism in the white highlands:

> London is quite mixed so that doesn't affect me much at the moment, but I do worry about when I go far away to a different city and they might be all white and they might have protests against other colours. Because you see in London you don't really have much racism but I know that there is racism in other places that aren't so mixed.

Here Wing has more in common with contingent than with em-bedded choosers. Even so she would not stay 'just because I want to stay, it is more the better university I would go to'. Her parents 'would prefer me to stay at home' and they have been saving to help her financially. 'They will support me anyway. I think they have kind of got the financial means to do so'. But they do not know the English education system, 'so it is just like I am by myself'. Wing does not possess Navid's transnational cultural capital and the social capital deployed by other embedded choosers is not so readily to hand and has to be worked at with a degree of strategic design. She has to improvise but she does manage to secure and later take up a place at LSE.

Ethnic Mix

We saw that a number of the minority students interviewed took the ethnic mix of the universities they considered applying to into account in their decision making. Of the 65 minority student tran-scripts analysed, 25 students indicated ethnic mix as a factor they had taken into account; 34 stated that this was not a concern or made no mention of it; the remaining four made vague references to 'mix'. State and private and school-age and mature students were all represented among those for whom ethnic mix was an issue, and students from the full range of minority ethnicities were included. Overall however, the FE and CCS students, those from mainly working class backgrounds, were more likely to identify ethnic mix as a concern (11) than the private, MU or RC students. The RC students seemed least concerned (2). To reiterate, ethnic mix was one among a variety of choice criteria in play but could be a decisive factor in not ruling out certain universities or types of universities or areas of the country as possible choices. The relevance of ethnic mix within choice begs questions about the nature of ethnic identity. For all but two or three students it would probably be accurate to say that their ethnic identity, as displayed or called up in the choice of higher education, is as Modood, Beiston and Virdee (1994, p119) argue, 'a plastic and changing badge of membership' which is located 'in a wider set of linked identities' (p117):

> ... ethnic identities are not simply 'given' or fixed over time. The field of ethnic minority identities in Britain indeed displays the context-dependent and to some extent interest-dependent characteristics of identity. (Modood *et al*, 1994, p6)

For some students choice was partly about sustaining aspects of their ethnic identity or having this identity valued and defended or at least not having to defend or assert the value of their identity. Some higher education contexts were seen as more tolerant of difference or, perhaps more accurately, these were contexts where difference and diversity were normal. Settings of diversity potentially offer an escape from essentialism, from fixity, and allow for the possibility of play across a variety of identities; the making and re-making of identity. Nonetheless, as Gillborn (1995) points out, fluidity can fix very quickly. In contrast there are those contexts – where particular ethnicities predominate – in which either identity becomes fixed in relation to the prevailing norm (whatever that might be) or in which there is a strong possibility of being positioned as other. There are, or appear to these students to be, different possibilities for identity in different sorts of settings and concomitantly different risks of marginalisation[8]. Candice, who is dual heritage/Black British, from the MU consortium, was wary of Warwick on these grounds:

> I'm very conscious that the attraction for me of staying in London is the racial mix you get at even some of the top universities, you know, that one of the main reasons for choosing London would be

my racial background. I did notice how white Warwick was and that did make me feel a bit uncomfortable, like I was an outsider.

Amrit, a Bangladeshi student from CCS, made the same point:

I don't care if there are lots of different ethnic backgrounds and stuff, people from different ethnic backgrounds, that doesn't bother me. As long as it is mixed with all sorts of people there, not just white ... I'd want it to be all mixed but I can get along with anyone, basically, the colour or what race they are, that doesn't bother me.

Deborah, from CCS, whose parents are Nigerian, picks up the other aspect of this in her contrast between 'mix' and 'swamping':

My friend, who is Nigerian. I think basically there is a lot more Nigerians that go there [Oxford Brookes] than, say, Leeds or whatever. You know, how you get one ethnic minority dominating another, in comparison to another place, and she goes, I mean, she didn't say it was swamped with Nigerians, but she said that you do get quite a lot. You could probably pick out seven or eight Nigerian students, you know, every day or something like that.

When asked if this was important to her, she went on to say: 'I wasn't really too bothered about that. It was really nice to know, yeah, there are Nigerian students there, so I liked that about it but it doesn't really matter'. What seemed to be of issue for almost all these students, to different degrees of significance, was mix or diversity rather than the presence of significant numbers of students of the same ethnicity as themselves. The latter would have the potential effect of foregrounding ethnic identity as against other dimensions of identity. Diversity offers the potential, as these students see it, of backgrounding ethnicity.

For the white students we interviewed ethnic mix was not a concern, at least not one that they shared with us, either in positive or negative terms (with two exceptions – see below). There was certainly no indication of anything like an ethnic identity at work in relation to choice-making. Although mix could have been an issue if what were described as 'ethnic universities' were being considered. When it did elicit a response from white students, the question of social mix was interpreted either in terms of social class or – more vaguely, but also perhaps class related – in terms of the intelligence and interests of other students[9]. This may be no surprise and its absence has its own significance. Various researchers and commentators have noted:

> ...the identity of white culture is 'absent' in a number of senses, both political and subjective ... An identity based on power never has to develop consciousness of itself as responsible, it has no sense of its limits except as those are perceived in opposition to other. (Pajackowska and Young, 1992, p202)

Nonetheless, it would be difficult to see all the white students in our sample as inhabiting 'an identity based on power' within the field of higher education choice. Social class remains as a major fault line in patterns of higher education participation (see chapter 1). Only two students articulated an awareness of white ethnicity. Both represent interesting confirmation of the point made by Pajackowska and Young. Simon, a private school student, described his school as 'almost run' by the Jews 'with the Asians' and opined that 'you almost feel like a minority being white'. He was 'looking forward' to going to University (York) 'to experience being in the majority'. Within the context of almost feeling like a minority, Simon has developed a consciousness of himself as white. The only mention of the negative connotations of the ethnic mix of universities, made by a white student, Lucy, was a reference to 'swamping' and not dissimilar to Simon's concern:

> To be honest I don't like to feel swamped, that I'm on my own sort of. Like I wouldn't like to be where it's mostly Black. I'm a bit worried about King's, my mum said one of their colleges is down in Brixton and I don't want to feel scared. Do you know what I mean? I'm not racist but I want a mix that's not all Black like here. I don't want to be outnumbered.

The other references to the impact of ethnic minority representation in universities came from ethnic minority students who were worried either about the predominance of certain ethnic minority groups in particular institutions (as above) or the status implications of having a degree from an 'ethnic university'. Annas, a mature student, who is Jordanian, explained that:

> I applied for South Bank University, my personal opinion, I think it is good in computing, but it has the reputation somehow of being an ethnic university and I think that is not good for getting jobs afterwards.

And Candice commented that

> ... everyone just everyone said don't apply to London Metropolitan. It's a fact of life as a Black person that you're going to be judged harshly there's no point in making life more difficult for yourself by going somewhere everyone sees as no good if you don't have to. It wasn't just school, all my friends and my mum's friends said 'just don't do it'. Also I met someone at the University of East London who said it was virtually impossible, really really difficult to get into law as a Black female from an old Poly. You are just automatically going to be seen as second rate.

The comments made about ethnic mix in the vignettes above, plus others, are discussed below. The responses of the minority students fall into three rough and ready categories: those who are de-racialised choosers, for whom ethnic mix is not part of their thinking about university choice; those who are race aware, who have thought about ethnic mix but for whom this is not a major factor in their choices; and those, a small minority, who are race active, for whom ethnic mix is a significant factor, among others, in choice making. Sheila, who is Black British and from MU, is a good example of someone who is race aware:

> I would say that using this school as an example, there aren't a lot of Black people in this school. And I think I've got on quite well despite that. It doesn't bother me. I am not one of those people that sit there and think – oh, I'm Black and there's all these white people around me. I just get on with it basically. It doesn't bother me, as long as I don't face any kind of discrimination, which I haven't faced in this school. Everyone just accepts you as you are, do you know what I 'mean? So I just get on with it. I don't think it's going to be a problem.

Elizabeth and Navid, quoted earlier, would fit this category, whereas Temi (Nigerian CCS) and Hinal (Indian CB) represent aspects of the race active category. Temi has a view that racism is more likely to be experienced in particular locations – the white highlands – and this is transmitted via grapevine knowledge:

> I: And you talked about your brother saying Kent's not a good university because it is very white. Is that an issue in relation to the other universities?
>
> Temi: Not really because I've mostly applied to universities that have a mix of different cultures. I think Middlesex, London Metropolitan, they're quite mixed. Brighton he did say it was quite a few

white people, mostly white people but not racist like Kent. Anyway I am used to that kind of area, I used to be down there ...

Hinal had lived in Newcastle and his experience had convinced him not to choose a provincial university. He wanted to stay in London:

> Well, we had a lot of like, dad's friends and my friends were there, but I suppose, this kind of sounds really hard to say, but some people were quite racist in the neighbourhood. And in fact, we actually went there to see the old house, and my brother was driving and we stopped the car to let these people walk past, and they shouted out racist slurs, and this was in our neighbourhood, where we used to live, so when I am driving through that place, or my brother's driving, but it just occurred to me that I wouldn't want to stay there again.

Jamaal, whose views were presented earlier, exemplifies this more clearly. His Islamic identity and sense of community was a key factor in his higher education applications. Laura, Cassie, Helen and Wing, and in a different way Candice and Annas, all quoted earlier, are race active. In contrast Sabrina, an Iranian young woman (MU), did not see mix or racism as issues for her: 'university is sort of where mature people go, I don't think they would be like that!' (cf. Osler, 1999). Navid, Kurram (Bangladeshi RC) and Vishal (Indian RC) evince more strongly a desire to escape their ethnic peers and distance themselves from an identity which is predicated or mainly founded upon their ethnicity. They are perhaps, in Cote's (1996) terms, 'dis-investing' in one sort of identity capital and 're-investing' in another sort, or as Beck (1992) would put it, they are making their biographies into a reflexive project. Kurram and then Vishal explained:

> I don't hardly have any Asian friends at all, because I've kept it that way. Not because I don't like them, but I prefer not to be in such a big Asian group. Because I just don't like it.

> That's the main point in coming here (RC), really, to get away from, because like, where I live, mostly Asians. So I thought I'd come here to get a different view of life. It's been a good experience ... It makes me think I wouldn't mind [what university] because I think I'll make friends with different sorts of people...

Even those ethnic minority students who are race active or race aware still see ethnic mix as only one factor among several in their decision making and a number of these end up selecting and then deciding to attend institutions which are predominantly white. There are dangers in a uni-focused analysis. While ethnicity may be a significant feature in the higher education choices of some minority students, it is not necessarily crucial or predominant for most. It does not tell us everything we need to know about choice. Nonetheless, it would be a useful exercise to follow up these different perceptions and concerns and choices in relation to patterns of degree completion (see Bird, 1996 and Osler, 1999).

Another variation of race active choosing occurs in the decision making of some of the Jewish students in our sample; although only four of the 16 viewed their Jewishness as having a bearing upon their choice of university. For these four, the existence of a significant Jewish student community at university was an attraction; for three of the four this meant, as Helen from HG put it, 'a good Jewish social life'. Lydia, from RC, selected all her UCAS choices by combining league table rankings of law departments with the guide to campus life provided by the Union of Jewish Students. Even here though, things are not straightforward. Lydia avoided Manchester because, as she put it: 'it's full of Beckys'. She put Nottingham as her first choice. However, as in the case of other minority students, ethnic identity for Jewish students was plastic, changing, interlinked and context dependent. Anne, another HG student, explained: 'I quite like it when there's a mix ... Because I'm reform. I don't go to a shul or anything like that. I just, I just am Jewish. I don't really do anything'. Alexandra, also from HG, who taught Jewish Studies to young children, explained that 'my parents want me to apply to Leeds, it's got a very high Jewish population and my parents are keen on that' but went on to say 'It's not that important, it's not the deciding factor'. But exactly as in other ethnic groups there were other Jewish students for whom their own ethnicity was unimportant to them in their sense of themselves and their choice making.

Ethnicity, class and class fractions

Throughout this chapter we have stressed the ways in which ethnicity is enmeshed in wider issues of culture which include class. Fitting in and feeling comfortable are often dependent on a complex compilation of factors. These, while incorporating ethnicity, are much broader, as Kalok demonstrates when he tries to explain why he turned down an offer from Cambridge; a place he says all his friends thought he was mad to refuse:

> It was a complete shock, it was different from anywhere else I have ever been, it was too traditional, too old fashioned, from another time altogether. I didn't like it at all. It was like going through a medieval castle when you were going down the corridors. The dining room was giant long tables, pictures, it was like a proper castle, and I was thinking – where's the moat, where's the armour? Save me from this. You know, you expect little pictures with eyes moving around, watching you all the time. And I just didn't like the atmosphere, not one bit.

You get a sense in Kalok's words that Cambridge is worlds away from his experience not only spatially but temporally too. And while part of his aversion stems from the whiteness of Oxbridge – he says that he felt 'as if he was the only brown face there' – you also get a powerful sense of the alienation of class cultural differences.

The differences which were evident among the minority students in our study cannot be adequately conveyed without reference to social class. Essentially the contingent/embedded division is class based. For those represented here as contingent choosers, the decision to attend university and obtain a degree has a specific class meaning in addition to, and interwoven with, its implications for ethnic identity. Giddens' (Beck, Giddens and Lash, 1994, p74) representation of choice as 'obviously something to do with colonising the future in relation to the past ...', is apt. For contingent choosers, as discussed in the previous chapter, going to university involves their becoming a person different from the rest their family and many of their peers, in eschewing a normal biography and at the same time risking a sense of feeling themselves out of place, even if they 'fulfil the conditions that the space tacitly requires of its occupants' (Bourdieu, 1999b, p128). As Bourdieu and Passerson put it in a much earlier study: 'to want to be, and to want to choose one's identity, is, first of all, to refuse to be what one has not chosen to be' (1979, p38).

This is equally true of ethnic and class aspects of identity for the minority working class students in this study, although for a few of them their choice of higher education is framed by an attempt to retain a fixed ethnic identity. It is equally apparent that some others are working upon themselves to disentangle themselves from an ethnic identity and a sense of community. There are similarities here with the solidarist and individualist class fractions we discussed in chapter 5. For the Bangladeshi working class students in CCS it is extremely important to hold on to their ethnic identity, whereas for a number of the other ethnic minority students it is seen as something to struggle free of. Whether this is always possible is another matter. Some ethnic minority students, particularly those from working class backgrounds, risk alienation and isolation (see Bird, 1996), much in the way described by Jackson and Marsden (1962).

However, this is not simply a matter of existential discomfort. Ozga and Sukhnandan (1998, p321), in a study of higher education non-completers, relate non-completion to 'lack of preparedness for university life – inadequate sources of information and unrealistic expectations and compatibility of choice'. That is 'the degree of match between students and their choice of institution and course' (p322). First generation choosers without appropriate cultural capital or relevant social capital may easily find themselves in the wrong place or in the wrong course, with all the risks of drop-out that that brings into play. Indeed, half of the ten universities with the highest drop-out rates also have high proportions of ethnic minority students (HEFCE figures). Some of the choices made by some of the contingent choosers were haphazard to say the least. Moogan, Baron and Harris (1999) also make the point that being able to draw upon direct, word of mouth, 'experience qualities' in decision making about higher education is a 'risk reducing strategy'. As we have seen, access to such grapevine knowledge is unevenly distributed, as are the time and resources available to commit to information and knowledge gathering and accessing professional support structures and expertise, and such support was differently available in the institutions in our study.

Alongside these personal and social dimensions of choice, for many contingent choosers the direct financial costs and opportunity costs of higher education study are a considerable burden. Hesketh (1999) found that working class students were least happy about and least likely to take out a loan. Typically such students are required to live at home, minimise the costs of travel and work part time during term time. This not only creates a different kind of higher education experience but again produces risks in terms of course performance and completion.

In contrast to all this, we see the embedded students moving into a class setting in which they feel comfortable, although it may be that some over-estimate the racial tolerance and social mixing within university settings (Osler, 1999). Going into higher education is a natural progression, part of a well-established normal biography. Cultural and social capital are in good supply and make the process of choosing into a vivid experience that is set in relation to longer-term planning and expectations. Costs are not an issue, working in term time is not expected and is often actively discouraged by parents. Moving away from home is seen by many as part of the experience of higher education and these students were the only ones to talk about extra-curricular activities at university. They know what to expect and what opportunities they might take advantage of. But class is an issue here in another sense. For middle class ethnic minority students from state schools, like their white peers, Oxbridge is class-different. It is 'posh', it is 'private school'. They do not feel comfortable there as they do in other university settings.

Concluding comments

Choice is inappropriate but useful as a conceptualisation of the decision making processes examined here. Inappropriate because of its tendency to emphasise individual preferences but useful in reminding us that this decision making is a set of practices – the key point is that we must retain the link between constraint and volition (James, 1996), and between dispositions and possibilities. Related to such a view of choice, Beck (1992, p131) makes the argument that:

> Class differences and family connections are not really annulled in the course of individualisation processes. Rather, they recede into the background relative to the newly emerging 'center' of the bio-

graphical life plan ... from knowing one's 'class' position one can no longer determine one's personal outlook, relations, family position, social and political ideas or identity.

In relation to university choice, as indicated in chapter 5, he is both right and wrong. Right in so far as contingent choosers are planning a biography that involves a kind of break with family and class, and in some cases, ethnic background, although on the other hand many of them end up staying at home. Wrong in as much that class still has a great deal to tell us about outlook, relations and identity particularly in relation to the continuities of life-planning and strategies of closure which were evident among the embedded choosers. However, having argued for the centrality of class divisions in higher education choice and having established patterns of commonality across ethnicities but within class groups, we are not suggesting that class commonalities are absolute nor that class washes out ethnic difference. The class experiences of different ethnic groups are likely to be different in terms of structures of feeling and subjectivity and the possibilities of agency. Different kinds of historical relationships to British capitalism and Empire may well produce different textures in the lived experience of class.

Increasingly, the relevant questions to ask about both ethnicity and class in relation to higher education are not just about who goes? but also who goes where? and why? In the next chapter we return to the entire sample in order to consider the information, both formal and informal, that higher education applicants utilise in their choice making.

Notes

1 The terminology used in the chapter to describe the individual students draws upon their preferred nomenclature. We are very aware that categories of ethnicity are socially constructed and contested and change frequently (see Mason, 2000 and Bonnett and Carrington, 2000). The generic shorthand minority is used here to refer to all the Jewish, dual-heritage and non-white students in our sample. It is recognised nonetheless that minority is as much a statement of power relations as it is a statistical observation; although here, as will be seen, these power relations are immensely complex. As is evident in the discussion in the chapter, the salience of ethnicity as a component of social identity varies considerably across the sub-sample. We are also very much aware of the problematic constitution of minority here. The minority subject is 'irretrievably heterogeneous' (Spivak, 1993, p.79). Or to look at it another way 'white' itself is neither unitary nor unproblematic (Bird, 1996 p97). Welsh, Scottish, Irish,

Hungarian, Polish, German are just some of the 'identities' not included here but represented in our full sample. The point is that the lines of demarcation could have been drawn differently. Nonetheless, we would suggest that, given the nature of our findings, the overall thrust of the arguments in the chapter would not have been altered significantly

2 As explained below, the differences here are strongly class-related and differentiate working class from middle class students across our sample as a whole. The concern with ethnic mix is however almost exclusively limited to the minority ethnic students.

3 As a reminder:

> An ideal type is formed by the one-sided accentuation of one or more points of view and by the synthesis of a great many diffuse, discrete, more or less present and occasionally absent concrete individual phenomena, which are arranged according to those one-sidedly emphasised viewpoints into a unified analytical construct. (Shils and Finch, 1949 p90)

4 See chapter 4.

5 Parents, and mothers in particular, were most broadly engaged in support of the lower or novitiate middle class embedded choosers but least involved among the private school choosers. For the latter the levels of support and organisation within the schools obviated the necessity for much practical engagement from parents. As within several other issues identified in the chapter, this flags up the significance of class fractional differences within the middle class.

6 It is worth thinking about this in more than one way. The failure to visit universities is a problem of cost and organisation and confidence for these students – the private schools and MU organised programmes of visits. But this is also a problem of knowing what to look for. When they do talk about the universities they are interested in it is often in terms of the facilities, a concrete but also safe version of the institution – buildings, rooms, equipment. What else is there to see? The maintaining of a distance from the universities may also be in part an issue about knowing how to behave, how to look and act like – embody – a university student – an issue of habitus.

7 Socioscapes are 'networks of social relations of very different intensity, spanning widely different territorial extents...' (Albrow, 1997, p.51).

8 This is different from the findings of Modood et al (1997) which indicate that in the main minorities expressed an ethnic preference were more interested in the presence of their own group than the presence of other ethnicities, in relation to schools (p320-323) and neighbourhood (p189-190). The difference between those findings and ours may well be related to age and context, and social class, as well as to the location of the research. The arguments put here are intended to be specific in these senses rather than general.

9 Osler (1999 p56) reports that the minority students she interviewed found their experiences of exclusion as complex, especially 'when other factors such as social class or gender stereotyping come into play'.

7

Illuminating the field? Information, marketing and higher education decision making

I n this chapter we consider the information, both formal and informal, that higher education applicants use in their decision making. Fully to understand the information processing students and their families engage in, we also look briefly at the marketing strategies of higher education providers. One section of the questionnaire we gave to the students was devoted to asking them what sources of information they were using to help them choose. School/college, prospectuses, higher education establishments, friends and career advisors were all selected by over half of the 502 respondents as sources of information they used a lot. A third of students were using fathers for information and slightly more (36%) saw their mother as an important source of information. Slightly less than a third were drawing on siblings for advice while just over a quarter of respondents said websites were a useful source of information.

However, the main foci of the chapter are the practices of applicants, the tactics they employ, their readings and misreadings of universities, and the social differences and divisions that result from the enormously varied quantity and quality of social, cultural and economic capital among the sample. While the dominant model of decision making is still that of rational choice theory in which students are perceived to be rational decision makers, our data, particularly that from in-depth qualitative interviews, indicates that decision making is often a messy process in which intuition, affective response and serendipity can play as great a role as systematic evaluation and careful consideration of the evidence available.

Marketing higher education

Writing about the US higher education market, Wesley Shumar (1997) argues that:

> Marketing and advertising of colleges threaten to produce a system of highly prestigious sought-after institutions in high demand, a second layer of less illustrious institutions doing their best to imagine themselves illustrious and a huge number of institutions using all the market techniques they can get their hands on to sell their product to a consuming public. (p134)

The same stratifying processes are evident in the marketing strategies of UK universities. Institutions like Oxford, Cambridge, Bristol, King's College London, Durham, LSE and Imperial trade on their exclusivity, fostering images which foreground tradition, esteem and academic distinction. Great reliance is placed on the prospectus, which is always tasteful, understated yet illustrious, deploying traditional iconography which stresses history and academic precedent. Most of this work of self fabrication (Jamieson, 1984) is directed towards a nostalgic attempt to regain a missing past (p66). Hi-tech, glossy images are utilised to conjure up the idea of a university that is not primarily about the high-tech and glossy but rather about a set of values which have an established, elite and exclusive history (Ball, 2000). For these universities exclusivity is still the product on offer and it is that, in the guise of classicism and traditionalism, which is being tastefully packaged and offered to the discerning consumer.

In contrast, at the other end of the market, many of the new universities promote themselves as accessible, with wide appeal, and emphasise social aspects of university life as much if not more than academic aspects. Yet this focus on the student, rather than the academic, culture can have counterproductive consequences:

> When we went to Manchester Met they took us up to a room and the first thing they showed us was a video about the social life of Manchester Met. And you know it was just such a contrast and I sat there thinking what are these people doing? Are they trying to get us to go to this university? And they showed us the social life and we saw people drinking. I know students do that anyway but I just think it was a good way of putting us off. (Esther, Black African middle class student)

Prospectuses and open days are supplemented with heavy sell to prospective consumers. In London, and other large cities, adverts for new universities proliferate – in tubes, the back of buses, the side of taxis and in the cinemas. In the field of higher education just as in the promotion of consumer goods such as food and furniture, 'it is as much about establishing familiarity, authority and legitimacy as it is about establishing difference' (Brierley, 1995, p142). The higher education brand leaders, Oxbridge, King's, LSE and Imperial do not need brand advertising like the new entrants into the field of higher education, Middlesex, South Bank, Greenwich, because they have well established authority and credibility. However, our research indicates that the new universities are trapped in a double bind in which their current marketing strategies militate against, rather than work towards, the gaining of legitimacy and credibility. For the most part, their tactics are directed at reinforcing and elaborating their existing identities. Although a significant minority of students remained unaware of advertising, among those who were aware the general consensus was that universities should not need to advertise if they are good:

> I see advertising as a sign of maybe their application rate is quite low, that they're getting a bit desperate. (Carl, Black working class student, RC)

> If I've noticed adverts at all it has been to put me off. I don't want to go somewhere that's pleading for me to go there. (Shera, dual heritage middle class FE student)

> It makes them seem a bit crap really. (James, white working class student, CCS)

> I mean to me it is like the university must be really desperate to be advertising on the Northern line, trains and stuff like that so I wouldn't go, no way. (Deborah, African middle class student, CCS)

For many students, including Carl, Shera, Deborah and James, advertising was synonymous with begging – it reeked of desperation, low standards and a lack of academic distinction that no emphasis on student culture and social life could disguise. Just how this lack of academic distinction is linked to advertising is made explicit in the narrative of Mrs Ginsberg, a Jewish middle class mother:

> My dread at first when Helen was refusing to listen to us is that she'd unwittingly go to what is an old polytechnic, not knowing that there might be a different quality of students there as well, so she would be with a peer group who would bore her and be well below her standard. There wouldn't be any standards to speak of if they were polytechnics before and also the way these places still draw in students. You know, some of them actually advertise on the television.

But not all the students were deterred by advertising:

> The only advertising I can actually remember is for Middlesex University, all the time, all over the train and I actually looked at Middlesex when I started thinking about universities because I'd seen so many adverts. (Jade, white working class student, MU)

> I think it makes them more easily accessible – the advertising, so you know – I'll just phone up the number or whatever. (Chaka, Asian middle class student, RC)

However, across the overall sample advertising had a detrimental impact on how universities were viewed by students. Slightly more than half of the students were aware of advertising, and of these, two-thirds found adverts off-putting rather than appealing.

Prospectuses
By far the most widely used source of information cited by both the mature students and the younger students and their parents were universities' own prospectuses. However, while all the institutions had banks of prospectuses in their careers libraries, the state school sixth formers seemed to have largely acquired their copies through attending higher education fairs organised through the LEA:

> I went home from the higher education fair with three bags full of prospectuses. My back was killing me. (Deirdre, Irish working class student MU)

> We all collected masses of prospectuses and I ended up with loads. (Aba, dual heritage middle class student, MU)

> I went to the universities fair day and lugged about 17 prospectuses home with me. (Sophie, white middle class student, HG)

> I got all the prospectuses from the higher education fair, masses of them. Plus my friends gave me all of theirs as well because they went to some other higher education fair and they got loads as well. (Sarah, dual heritage working class student, MU)

However, regardless of the means of acquisition, all 120 students interviewed had consulted them and opinion was largely positive:

> I mostly looked at prospectuses. I found those the most helpful. (Chemtas, dual heritage, middle class student, MU)

> The key advice was the library of prospectuses. (Frank, white, middle class, CB)

> I found the prospectuses most helpful really. (Julia, white working class FE student)

> The prospectuses were most helpful because they were more detailed. (William, white middle class student, MU)

Yet although prospectuses were widely viewed as very helpful, as Connor *et al* (1999) found, they were often viewed as promotional documents and many were seen as lacking sufficient detail about their courses. But a few of the students, apart from making cursory consultations of the UCAS handbook, had been totally dependent on prospectuses for information. These students were primarily those who were time poor (Ball *et al*, 1997), and were concentrated in the FE college and CCS. As Khorul and Alomgir, two working class Bangladeshi students at CCS, pointed out 'you need a free day to do any research other than go through the prospectuses and we haven't got a spare day available'; while Nathan, an English, working class FE student, emphasised that 'it's really difficult finding the time. The access course is so intensive, it's a problem taking time out from that and I can't afford to take a day off work'. However, students at the other state institutions were also heavily reliant on prospectuses for information:

> Prospectuses were the only way of making my decision. I haven't used anything else. I haven't visited the unis at all so the prospectuses helped a great deal. (Margaret, Black British working class student, MU)

I didn't really go to any of the universities. I just took judgement on the prospectuses. (Pardeep, Indian middle class student, RC)

I just looked at the prospectuses. (Kalok, Chinese, working class student, MU)

There were a number of dissenting and more discerning voices amongst the barrage of positive response and over dependency. Sometimes the criticisms related to the kind of dumbing down referred to earlier in relation to advertising:

You can tell what the universities are like, when they have their prospectus trying to make it look like some kind of youth magazine, it puts you off. (Jack, white middle class student, MU)

One of the universities presented their prospectus as a magazine and that was quite confusing. (Mark, white middle class student, RC)

At other times interviews highlighted the ways in which traditional iconography could be deployed in prospectuses in ways which, while not actively deceiving, could subtly mislead the reader (Maguire *et al*, 1999):

There was a student whom I thought there were quite a lot of courses at Greenwich which would suit her well and she was – 'what sort of place is Greenwich?' – you know, very suspicious. And I went and found the prospectus and once I'd found that picture of what used to be the Royal Maritime Museum, she went 'Oh, that's alright then'. (Mrs Walters, careers advisor, RC)

A handful of students, nearly all male and middle class, were uniformly negative:

Prospectuses give you nothing about the universities, over exaggerate and they are just useless really. It's just you don't learn anything about them. They could change the name on the front and you wouldn't realise in the slightest because they are just all pretty much the same. And I didn't find them very useful at all. (Jake, white middle class student, MU)

After a bit you sort of glaze over because everywhere claims they are exciting and innovative and you want to be there. So after your fourth glossy brochure you sort of think- ugh, where are the differences? (Frank, white middle class student, CB)

What both Jake and Frank are complaining about is a perceived lack in prospectuses of hard as opposed to soft information. As Tim articulates: 'in the prospectuses it's all nice and glossy, it doesn't actually have hard information on departmental things, it doesn't have comparisons to every other university department'.

The three have to search elsewhere for the sort of information they see as essential in their decision making. A number of parents expressed similar views about the limitations of prospectuses:

> I think you have to read between the lines. I think prospectuses are only good for getting things like entrance requirements, that background sort of stuff, they are not decisive kind of information. (Mrs Adams, white middle class mother)

> Some things we only really picked up on the visits. We found things out that hadn't really come across in the prospectus. I don't think the prospectuses actually give a brilliant idea of what it's really about. (Mrs Marcusan, white middle class mother)

They also highlight, as Mrs Adams makes explicit, that information in the prospectuses is far from transparent, requiring the complex decoding skills that comes with the particular kinds of cultural capital that characterised middle class rather than working class families. In fact a small number of middle class families in this study engaged in processes of sophisticated sorting and ranking based on prospectuses. Such families employed a kind of hyper-rational model of information processing far removed from the *ad hoc*, serendipitous approach of many working class students.

Guides

Only a small minority (about twenty) of the students talked about making use of guides to universities in their choice making, although careers staff at SH, CB and RC all mentioned that guides were kept in the Careers department as a resource for students:

> They like the Push guide which gives a sort of view of the university as a social place to be. It tells you the price of beer and those sorts of things. We've got the Potter guide which I think the sensible one to use because that does say what kind of campus it is and what kind of city it is, and sensible information. But they love the Push guide, so that's ok, if they're trying to make their minds up it's one other thing. (Mrs Walters, Careers teacher RC)

However, none of the students mentioned either the Push or the Potter guide. Most frequently mentioned was the *Virgin Guide*, followed by the *Which* and the *Good University Guide*:

> We had the *Virgin Guide*. It was very useful. (Mrs Adams, white middle class mother)

> I looked at the *Virgin Guide* for social life. (Jake, white, middle class student, MU)

A few families looked at everything available:

> We looked at all the alternative guides. (Mrs Fergerson, white middle class mother)

> We've got guides at home. We just brought book after book. (Emily, white middle class student, HG)

Three of the Jewish students mentioned drawing on guides devised specifically for Jewish students:

> I still have very big links with an organisation called the Association of Jewish Sixth Formers and they have a campus guide which they send out every year ... some of the Jewish people I know are so well informed about where they are going to university just because we've got such a support system. (Helen, Jewish middle class student, HG)

Consulting guides also seemed to be a predominantly middle class activity. Only one working class student talked about using guides in her decision making:

> Basically I found things out from magazines and we looked at the best university guides in the bookshops and stuff like that because there's a big Books Etc just up the road from me and there are sofas, so you can just go and look at them, you don't have to buy them. So all my information about those sorts of things is from Books Etc. (Lorna, white working class student, MU)

Explicit in Lorna's text is a probable reason why it was mainly middle rather than working class students who mentioned consulting guides – the cost.

Visits

Visits to universities were used far less often than prospectuses in students' decision making. This relates back to our earlier discussion of time poverty and the limitations lack of time placed on the options available to less materially advantaged students. As we have already seen, poorer students could rarely find the time to make visits as they juggled academic work and labour market commitments. In the FE college and CCS many students could also not afford the costs any more than the time involved:

> This issue about funding visits to open days is a big, big issue. We have actually, where students have expressed a real interest in going and seeing somewhere, we have actually tried to find the funds to cover half the cost of that where possible and in some circumstances that has been very difficult. We try and pay for half the train fare or coach fare and that's been a problem because students haven't got the money to do that. Parents haven't got the money to be able to send them on a trip and it's a big, big problem for many of our students. So although there have been trips available the uptake has been low. Even the Sussex trip, which was run jointly by the college and the school, I mean, it wasn't expensive, it was seven pounds, but still for some students that's unmanageable. (Sue, Head of Sixth Form, CCS)

The costs involved was also an issue for working class students in the other state institutions:

> I didn't get to see most of the universities that I applied to. That's one of the reasons I looked so carefully at the prospectuses and everything because I hadn't actually had a chance to see them. It's really expensive to go and visit universities all over the country. You need money. (Lorna, white English working class student, MU)

In the state institutions the visits which did occur were most often used post-UCAS as a mechanism of elimination rather than as part of a process of choice:

> So the open day is actually used by students for eliminating. Often it's only after they've been made an offer somewhere. It's at that stage they go. It's not 'let's have a look at universities and then I might make some choices'. They will say 'I'm going to Nottingham. I've had an offer and I want to see if I like the town'. (Ms Keen, 6th form coordinator, MU)

It was only in the two private schools that visits operated effectively as a means of choice making:

> Loads of people went on open days in the lower sixth. (Tim, white middle class student, CB)

> It all started with 'What are you doing?' 'Where are you going?' Went there, realised it existed. Then started filling in the UCAS form. (Louisa, white middle class student, HG)

Louisa spells out a different chronology to that of the majority of the state students. Their chronology would generally be one in which the order is reversed, with filling in the UCAS form coming before making visits – if any. Martin Rose, Head of MU's sixth form, implies that a significant minority of his students visit after they have made up their minds; a process of confirmation rather than elimination, and an event that is not only post UCAS – form filling but also post UCAS offer acceptance:

> It's mostly 'if they've made me an offer I'll go'. Or not even that. 'If I decide that's the one I want to go to then I'll visit it'. (Martin Rose, Head of Sixth Form, MU)

Yet visits, when time could be found for them, often made striking impressions and could prove central in the final choice of institution:

> I've been to Oxford and to be honest it's the only place that I felt I could be. I clicked with the place and I think that rare that you just find a place that you could really like. (Alicia, white middle class student, HG)

> To be quite honest with you, I think the thing that decided him on York was when he made a visit there and I think he kind of feel in love with the place. (Mrs Silvester, white middle class mother of RC student)

Again the lack of information and lack of direct experience prior to acceptance could be factors which are related to the non-completion of certain categories of students in certain sorts of institutions. This is not simply a matter of existential discomfort. As noted in chapter 6, in a study of higher education non-completers, Ozga and Sukhnandan (1998, p321), relate non-completion to 'lack of preparedness for university life – inadequate sources of information and unrealistic expectations and compatibility of choice'. That is 'the degree of match between students and their choice of institution and course' (p322).

Websites
Surprisingly, less than a third of the students had utilised computing resources in their decision making. Although even more surprising was Connor *et al*'s (1999) finding that less than 3 per cent of their 20,000 sample utilised IT-based media. For some of the

institutions, notably in the state sector this fairly low level of consultation seemed to be linked to resourcing:

> The booking system for computers is a real problem. You only have time to look at one university in the time allocated and that doesn't allow you to make any comparisons so it's a bit of a waste of time. (Khorul, CCS)

When the research project began in 1998, one of the state schools did not even provide access to the web:

> We are deficient in computers and I have been making a terrible fuss because we haven't got the internet yet. The vice principal has agreed that it is essential that we get it. We've only got one decent computer and four battered ones in careers. (Mrs Walters, RC)

In view of the inadequate school based provision it is hardly surprising that most accounts of web use referred to usage in the home where parents seemed to be consulting the net as much as their children:

> On the websites they give a bit more detail in terms of the course and how the courses operate. (Mrs Patterson, white middle class mother)

> My dad's been the one sitting there on the internet for hours printing off endless amounts of information for me to read through. (Katy Patterson, white middle class student, RC)

> We sat down with the league table and went through the internet to look through each and every single university that was doing the course he wants to do. (Mrs Caulrick, white middle class mother)

> She's gone onto university websites and it's been brilliant. (Mrs Milner, white working class mother)

> I printed out tons of those syllabuses from everywhere and that's when it came home that there actually was a material difference in where you went to study. And she realised that there were some courses that she thought were absolutely fascinating and some that were really dreary. Then I did the same for Cambridge and came up with two colleges which from the websites looked as if she would actually enjoy being there so I narrowed my choice to St Catherine's and Clare from the website. (Mrs Michaelson, white middle class mother)

Among the students themselves feelings were mixed as to the utility of the web in choice making:

> I started really nitty-gritty going onto the internet, onto their web pages and really finding out what it was like. (Alexa, white middle class student, HG)

> I did go to the SOAS website but it was exactly the same as the prospectus so its easier and cheaper to just flick through the book. (Julia, white working class mature student, FFEC)

> I literally went to all the websites and it was quite informative, you saw pictures but some of them were literally just photocopies of the prospectus. It was quite good for checking open day timings and dates but apart from that the only advantage was getting the e-mail address. (Navin, Indian middle class student, CB)

> The websites were completely useless, the ones that I looked at, so I just gave up after the first two. (Vicki, white working class student, RC)

> I did look at a few websites, they were just useless, didn't help at all. (Kalok, Chinese working class student, MU)

And a number of girls were self-deprecating about their ability to use the internet:

> The first time I went on the internet I thought I was going to kill the machine. I thought everything was going to go wrong and I had about three friends all helping me. (Louisa, white middle class student, HG)

> I did look at a few websites but not that much. I'm not really into the internet. I don't do that well on it. (Lisa, white working class student, MU)

> I'm not actually that competent at using the internet so... (Helen, white middle class student, HG)

The comments of both students and their parents suggest that universities are using the website differently. For some it remains simply electronic paper while others are attempting to utilise it as a real alternative medium.

League tables

> I checked the *Financial Times* website for the league tables and what I did was pick sort of three in the top twenty and I picked another two or three in the top forty. Birmingham was fourteenth

and Warwick was sixth or seventh. (Jonathon, white middle class student, RC)

While it was normative in the private schools to pay serious attention to league tables, Jonathon was one of only eighteen students in the state sector (just under a fifth of the total) to be guided by the league tables, another instance of the work of institutional habitus (Reay *et al*, 2000). Sue Adams, the Head of Sixth Form at CCS asserted that 'knowledge of the league tables is very foggy among our students', while Kath, an access tutor at FFEC, commented 'our students are much more inclined to listen to a friend who has been and enjoyed it...I think they take much more notice of things like that than actual league tables'. We discuss later the importance of peer networks but one consequence was the relatively low priority given to league tables among the state educated students. A common perspective amongst the state sector students was that of Amina: 'I haven't looked at any of the league tables' and Mark: 'I'm not really bothered if it's at the top of the league tables'. In part, this neglect of league tables as a source of information relates to the issues of class and ethnic aversion we have discussed in earlier chapters. For instance, Borbola reasons:

> I wouldn't like to go to a place where they might be first in every league table but there is no hands on experience only academic.

While Esther, who is middle class African, argues:

> The league tables might tell you which ones are most successful but it depends on what sort of individual you are because I could go to a top university and hate it, absolutely hate it and hate the people who go there, hate my tutors, hate the course because it's too traditional or I may go to a lower university and absolutely love it so I think it depends on what sort of person I am.

In contrast, the small minority of privileged families, we referred to earlier, were engaged in sophisticated processes of decoding information which included league table results as part of an array of data to be dissected:

> We certainly took league table results into account when we were looking at universities. But we didn't exclusively do that and we were looking at a lot of other factors as well, just like you do when you're looking at a school, you look at different aspects of it. We looked at accommodation, for example, what services were avail-

able. We looked at the quality of the library, what amenities were available... (Mrs Lindsay, white middle class mother)

Here we can see cultural capital in operation as the dispositions and skills to draw effectively on a wide range of sources of information.

Hot knowledge: friends and family as sources of information

Ball and Vincent (1998) found that in relation to secondary school choice, grapevine knowledge often took precedence over official information; that 'hot' knowledge was preferred to 'cold' official information. However, we found that it was primarily at the two ends of the social spectrum of our sample that grapevine knowledge was seen as more salient than official information. The young people at CCS and the mature students at FFC, often the first generation in their family to apply for higher education, placed a great deal of reliance on personal recommendations, for instance, people at bus stops; cousins etc. There are issues here about being outsiders to higher education which connect with a perceived need to fit in. For less privileged and first-time applicants the importance of soliciting the viewpoint of 'someone like me' led to the prioritising of hot over cold official knowledge; the latter often being seen to be constructed for more privileged applicants who are not subject to the same financial, time and distance constraints. Although the privately educated students also gave primacy to hot knowledge, the insider quality of the personal recommendations they were able to access meant their grapevine knowledge was of a totally different order to that of the far less well connected students at CCS and FFC:

> It wasn't so much the visits, it was actually because I talked to quite a few people, friends of the family who are doctors and they gave a lot of advice as well. It wasn't mainly from the school because the school can't tell you, they don't necessarily know what is the best place for each person. I found these friends who were doctors, their help was much more interesting. (Shamara, middle class Indian student, HG)

> My brothers helped me a lot and mates as well and I've got a lot of faith in what they say to me. School I don't know, I didn't really use the school. I didn't find that I needed that much because I've

got lots of help from outside ... My mum knows one of the people who works at one of the Cambridge colleges so she spoke to them and they gave her advice and stuff. (Jake, white Jewish middle class student, MU)

But Jake is in a privileged position shared by few of the other students at MU. His father is an eminent barrister and his mother a high ranking civil servant. While he can afford to bypass any services and advice the school provided, other students are more reliant on school and college based support. The hot knowledge they can access lacks the high cultural capital value of the informal information Jake is privy to.

Consequently, personal recommendations signify very differently within different class cultures. Elite upper middle class young people like Jake are able to contextualise personal recommendations within a whole spectrum of hard data; league table results and course content details, plus more reliable soft data such as family members' experiences. As Ball *et al* (1995) and David *et al* (1994) found in relation to secondary school choice, the middle classes tend to draw much more on multiple sources of information. Mrs Peterson exemplifies the cultural and social capital embedded in the upper echelons of the middle classes across both state and private sector schooling:

> But really the ones Marcus in thinking and talking about are the ones that are at the top of the list. And he thought and talked about them before we saw any lists. In a sense he just knew which the best ones were. And it wasn't the league tables. It's just a sense of the university, the location, the history, and just a kind of knowing that people just do know what's good. (Mrs Peterson, white middle class mother)

Mrs Peterson's words reveal how in the established middle classes higher education choice is not just a case of rational decision making but embodies a sense of academic distinction and exclusivity. Their habitus incorporates 'a feel for the game', an art of anticipating the future of the game which is inscribed in the present state of play (Bourdieu, 1998, p25). As Bourdieu points out (p81), such individuals surge ahead in the game because they have the immanent tendencies of the game in their body in an incorporated state: they embody the game. Individuals like Marcus, with his instinctive sense of the best, 'only have to let their habitus follow its natural bent in order to comply with the immanent necessity of the field and satisfy the demands contained within it' (Bourdieu, 1993, p76).

In stark contrast, mature working class students like Maureen talk about being swayed by a personal recommendation unsupported by any other evidence:

> It was actually the youth club manager who said that she'd gone to Reading and I should consider Reading. At that time I knew literally nothing about universities, the different types and everything so I just applied to Reading. (Maureen, Scottish working class FE student)

On being offered a place Maureen realises there is no possibility of being able to manage a degree course that requires commuting and the financial costs long distance travel involves, nor of juggling an intense academic course with her chronic domestic problems. Her situation is an extreme example, but many of both the mature and the younger working class students ended up placing more weight on personal recommendations than did their middle class counterparts. But at the same time they often lacked sufficient information from other sources – the sorts of social and cultural capital Marcus and his mother display – with which to appropriately contextualise any recommendations they received.

However, it is not simply an issue of class positioning. Dominant social and cultural capital is also a scarce resource for those students who are recent arrivals in Britain, regardless of class background. Such students are dealing in a currency which has become devalued through migration even if they were originally middle class in their country of origin (see Gewirtz et al, 1995; Reay, 1998b):

> I spent quite a lot of time in choosing, because, really because I didn't grow up in this country, I didn't know anything about any of the universities really. So I had to ask about people, ask around. Is this a good university or is this not? I kept on asking is this a good university is that a good university?(Borbala, Eastern European female refugee, FFEC)

and:

Filling in my UCAS form was a horrible situation. Because it was the first time I've ever applied to university, which was alright for everyone else, and like in my country there is no choice of university, there is only one that everyone is competing for. So I said – oh my God. All these universities, how am I going to choose from them. And then other people are saying – we are used to this, we have seen all these universities, we have heard of them. And me, I have only heard of one that was in my country. So this choice made me think – I can't do this. It's really hard for me. But then I say to myself you have to try and have to do it. You need to get to university to get on in this country. (Shillar, female African refugee, CCS)

Motaz, a young working class Black student whose parents migrated to Britain from Jordan, has included Hull among a list of new universities in London:

I: And the other thing I am interested in, because they are all London based apart from Hull, and the first time you applied you applied to Hull as well, so you are prepared to go out of London for a good course?

Motaz: Well Hull is a very good university.

I: So how did you find that out?

Motaz; Well first it was recommended to me by someone in the college. They told me it had a good reputation so then I looked at the prospectus and when I went to see the area, when I had an interview, it's a very nice area. I read a lot about it before I chose it. And it is a tourist attraction as well, the sea is not far from there. It has one campus only, many universities has different campuses. And it has been for a long time, it has a very good reputation. So that's why I chose it.

Later, when interviewing one of the college's careers advisors, she uses Motaz's experience to illustrate her point that many of the students would really prefer her to make the choice for them:

Recently there was a young man on the access to IT, he's actually one of our New Deal students, and he came to me and said, 'I've got an interview in Hull'. And I said 'that's interesting, why are you choosing Hull? And he said 'You said it was a good university'. I what? And I said 'I may have done, because I wouldn't have told you it was a bad one'... And he was going for an interview at Hull on the basis of whatever his notion was of 'Deirdre said it was good'.

Both Maureen and Motaz are making choices which turn out to be inappropriate for them, on the basis of fairly casual comments made by people they see as having superior knowledge and understanding to themselves of higher education.

Rachel Brooks (2005) found in her study of the role of friends and peers on young people's higher education choices in the UK that they rarely discussed their choice making with other young people. Schneider and Stevenson (1999) report that friends had a limited impact on either educational goals or career plan in the US context. We similarly found that young people overwhelmingly claimed not to be consulting, or even discussing, their choices with other students. This was in direct contrast to mature students, who regularly described higher education choice as a collaborative shared process. However, this is not to say that friends did not have an influence on young people's decisions regarding higher education. As we saw in chapter 3, there is an indirect influence that comes through institutional habitus. The institutional peer group provides a context for academic and social comparison, setting the parameters of what is possible in relation to higher education choice:

> I find that we all flow with each other. We don't follow each other because we are not sheep, but we tend to flow, and everyone tends to apply to these universities and then you think – do they do my course? Yeah, well, I'll have a look at that. And that is how it tends to go, so... It is sort of – oh, we are all going here, why don't you have a go and see if you like it, so you try it out and research it and if you like it you tend to follow that. (Omar, middle class Iranian student, CB)

As is evident in Omar's words, friends and peers exert a powerful influence on higher education choices despite many students' protestations that they are engaged in an individualised rather than a collective process. Just as we saw in chapters 3 and 4, what was frequently presented by the young students as a process of 'making my own mind up' was subject to pressures of collectivity. Sometimes overtly, at other times almost imperceptibly, friends, family and institution all inflect decision making.

Concluding comments

As Stephen Ball (2000) argues, the provision of information for consumers within the education market is linked to two main aspects of educational performativity – comparison and commodification. Both constitute different ways of making universities more responsive or appear more responsive to their consumers.

'There is a general tension or confusion in the education market between information-giving and impression management and promotion. This blizzard of hype, (pseudo) information and impression management also contributes to opacity rather than transparency' (Ball, 2000, p10).

It is against this background of increasing complexity and dissimulation and the growing marketisation and commodification of higher education that applicants are making their choices of higher education. However, here as in other aspects of higher education choice, we can see the workings of cultural and social capital operating to maintain and reinforce inequitable differences and distinctions. The middle class students not only have more hard information about universities and university courses, they also have access to hot knowledge that has a far higher currency and exchange value than the knowledge of their working class counterparts.

8

Conclusion

In contemporary Britain, within the transition from elite to mass higher education, a process of complex stratification and differentiation of HEIs has been created, replacing an earlier university system underpinned by relatively straightforward class-based inclusion and exclusion (Collins, 1999). While some institutions stand out, the majority compete for students, or for certain kinds of students in a fuzzy and changing hierarchy which is open to misreading and false moves. Students engage within this hierarchy in complex ways. We found little evidence of the consumer rationalism that predominates in official texts. There were some students who could be described as active researchers, especially at the two private schools, but many relied on serendipity and intuition. State school and working class pupils were likely to be selecting from one set of limited options (Reay *et al*, 2001b) and the private school students from another. Our data show that the experiences and expectations of applicants differ on the basis of social class, compounded by ethnicity and gender. There are clear differences within and between working and middle class groupings. Social class was found to be the main predictor of choosing high status universities, followed by qualifications and a career motive.

There are a number of constraints on the processes of choice: time for study and the importance of paid employment for the less affluent students. A third of students from the established middle classes were in paid employment compared with two thirds of students from unskilled households. On the other hand, many of the more affluent students were able to have extra tuition, increasing their chances of high A level achievement. Geographical constraints of travel and finance meant that working class students operated with limited choices among local universities. Most of the students from middle class backgrounds presented choice as taken-for-granted, inevitable – in contrast to the chancy, uncertain process recounted by many working class students. Class, linked to ethnicity, is also central to fitting in and feeling comfortable.

The use of information such as prospectuses, websites, open days, alternative guides and visits differed on the basis of social class. And the general consensus among the students interviewed was that universities should not need to advertise if they are good. A few students, primarily those who were time poor (Ball *et al*, 1997) and from the poorer institutions, were totally dependent on prospectuses for information. Consulting guides was a predominantly middle class activity, while it was only in the two private schools that visits operated effectively as a means of choice making. Yet visits, when time could be found for them, often made striking impressions and could prove central in the final choice of institution. Less than a third of the students had used computing resources in making their choice.

Sociologically speaking, choice – the implementation of practical knowledge – is a highly problematic concept. It threatens all sorts of theoretical and ontological difficulties and needs to be handled with great care. We have attempted here to construct the outlines of a sociology of higher education choice drawing on Bourdieu's theoretical tools. This allowed us to attend to choice as a social process, a process which is structured and structuring. That is, a process which is differentiated according to the distribution of relevant capitals and which plays its part in the re-institutionalisation of social divisions within higher education. Choice is rooted in fine discriminations and classificatory judgements of places for us and places for others – 'social structures in the head' as Bourdieu terms them. Within these social processes social class, ethnicity and in a different way gender all play their part but not in any mechanistic or simple sense. A sociological view of choice must recognise both obviousness (what people like us do) and necessity (the limitations of social and spatial horizons), and the complex and sophisticated nature of individual and familial decision making. In these respects, we, like others have found Bourdieu 'enormously good for thinking with' (Jenkins, 1992, p11) and have made extensive use of his conceptual framework, especially the concept of habitus: 'the practical mastery which people possess of their situations' (Robbins, 1991, p1). We found that higher education students were located in overlapping circles of individual, family, friends and institution but both institutional and familial habituses proved important in students' choices. These were closely aligned for the private school pupils, making for a fairly seamless process of choice (Reay *et al*, 2001a). In contrast, many state school students experienced a dissonance between home and school that rendered choice making more problematic.

We have argued through our data that the perceptions, distinctions and choices of universities made by students also plays its part in reproducing the divisions and hierarchies in higher education. For many middle class students who move in their world as a fish in water, going to, and choice of, university is simply what people like them do. Working class students, in contrast, were driven by necessity, which made certain choices unthinkable for them. Primarily, choosing to go to university is not really a choice at all for the middle classes students. It is about staying as they are and making more of themselves, whilst for the working classes it is about being different people in different places, about who they might be but also what they must give up.

The history of higher education in the UK continues to be overshadowed by class inequalities (Halsey, 1993; Blackburn and Jarman, 1993; Egerton and Halsey, 1993). It appears that the recent transition from elite to mass system of higher education has done little so far to erode class differentials in access, despite the concern which has been focused on the working class students who were previously excluded from higher education. In contrast, in relation to race, greater take up of university places proportionate to their white counterparts by ethnic minority students has been celebrated as a success story (Modood and Acland, 1998). In this book we have focused on the success stories – not only middle class white students but middle and working class ethnic minority applicants, and also white working class applicants to university who, considering the history of access to higher education in the UK, perhaps constitute even more of a success story. However, our findings reveal causes for concern as well as reasons for celebration. As our data vividly illustrates, the field of higher education is still far from a level playing field. Despite increasing numbers of working class students and particularly students from ethnic minority backgrounds, applying to university, their experiences of the choice process are for the most part qualitatively different to that of their more privileged middle class counterparts. Our data on such things as working in term time, living at home and problems of funding suggest that their experiences of higher education itself will be very different – different higher educations are on offer.

In our analysis the most powerful and pervasive issue to emerge is that of class and racial inequalities. The choice making of the middle class and working class students are very different and the higher educations they confront and anticipate are different and separate. Our data powerfully reveals that while more working class and ethnic minority students are entering university, they are generally entering different universities to their white middle class counterparts. Class tendencies are compounded by race. Just as most working class students end up in less prestigious institutions, so do most ethnic minority young people (Shiner and Modood, 2002). The combination and interplay of individual, familial and institutional factors produces very different opportunity structures (Roberts, 1993).

Our focus on choice of higher education signals a shift in the focus of attention in contemporary debates, as the higher education system itself moves from an elite to a mass system, from a concentration upon who goes and who does not go to University to questions about 'who goes where?' There is a political rhetoric of widening participation, 'fair' access, achievement-for-all and meritocratic equalisation within mass higher education. But this mostly ignores the consequences and opportunities which derive from going on to higher education – like different rates of completion, and returns in terms of income which are related to HEIs (Chevalier and Conlon, 2004).

In relation to the French educational system Bourdieu (1993, p97-8) wrote:

> There has been a devaluation as a simple effect of inflation, and also as a result of the change in the 'social quality' of the qualification holders. The effects of educational inflation are more complicated than people generally imply because a qualification is always worth what its holders are worth, a qualification that becomes more widespread is *ipso facto* devalued because it becomes accessible to people without social value.

His words seem slightly shocking but we argue that they have a powerful ring of truth, not just in relation to French universities but also in relation to UK higher education. Behind the very simple idea of a mass system of higher education we have to recognise a complex institutional hierarchy and the continued reproduction of racialised, gendered and classed inequalities in which universities are classified and judged by both the applicants themselves and wider society in accordance with their proportion of working class and ethnic minority intakes. Elitism is built into the very fabric of higher education whether elite or mass. Broadening the base of the student body will have little impact. In fact we would argue that very little will change until the ethos and culture of higher education radically alters. higher education is not the same experience for all, neither is it likely to offer the same rewards for all. As Valerie Walkerdine, Helen Lucey and June Melody assert: 'There is a creeping assumption ... that if we open up higher education to working class students then we can all become professionals. This is the biggest fiction of all' (Walkerdine *et al*, 2001).

References

Abbasi, K (1998) Is Medical School Selection Discriminatory? *British Medical Journal* 317, p1097-1098

Abrams, F (2003) Who's afraid of big bad debt? *Times Educational Supplement* 5 December 2003, p18

Albrow, M (1997) Travelling beyond local cultures, in J Eade (ed) *Living in the Global City* London: Routledge

Allatt, P (1993) Becoming Privileged: The Role of Family Processes in I Bates and G Riseborough (eds) *Youth and Inequality* Buckingham: Open University Press

Allatt, P (1996) Consuming Schooling: choice, commodity, gift and systems of exchange, in S Edgell, K Hetherington and A Warde (eds) *Consumption Matters* Oxford: Blackwell

Alwin, D F and Otto, L B (1977) Higher School Context Effects on Aspirations *Sociology of Education* 50, p 259-273

Anderson, C (1960) *Ministry of Education and the Secretary of State for Scotland Grants to Students: Report of the Committee Cmnd 1051* London: HMSO

Archer, L and Hutchings, M (2001) 'Bettering Yourself'? Discourses of risk, cost and benefit in ethnically diverse, young working class non-participants' constructions of higher education *British Journal of Sociology of Education* 22: 4 p555-575

Archer, L, Hutchings, M and Ross, A (2003) *Higher Education and Social Class: issues of exclusion and inclusion* London: RoutledgeFalmer

Arnot, M, David, M E and Weiner, G (1999) *Closing the Gender Gap: Post War Education and Social Change* Cambridge: Polity Press

Aschaffenburg, K and Maas, I (1996) Cultural and Educational Careers: The Dynamics of Social Reproduction. *American Sociological Review* 62, p573-587

Ball, S J (2000) Performativities and Fabrications in the Education Economy: Towards the Performative Society *Australian Educational Researcher* 27: 2, p1-23.

Ball, S J (2003) *Class Strategies and the Educational Market: the middle classes and social advantage* London: RoutledgeFalmer

Ball, S J, Bowe, R and Gewirtz, S (1995) Circuits of schooling: a sociological exploration of parental choice of school in social class contexts *Sociological Review* 43: 1, p52-78

Ball, S J, Maguire, M and Macrae, S (1997) The post-16 education market: ethics, interests and survival Paper presented at the Bera Conference University of York 11-14 September

Ball, S J and Vincent, C (1998) 'I heard it on the grapevine': 'Hot' Knowledge and school choice. *British Journal of Sociology of Education* 19: 3, p377-400

Ball, S J, Macrae, S and Maguire, M (1999) 'Young lives at risk in the 'futures' market: some policy concerns from on-going research in F Coffield (ed) *Speaking Truth to Power: Research and Policy in Lifelong Learning* Bristol: Policy Press

Ball, S J, Maguire, M and Macrae, S (2000) *Choice, Pathways and Transitions Post-16: new youth, new economies in the global city* London: Falmer

Barber, T (2002) A Special Duty of Care: exploring the narration and experience of teacher caring *British Journal of Sociology of Education* 23, p383-396

Beck, U (1992) *Risk Society: Towards a New Modernity* Newbury Park, CA., Sage

Beck, U, Giddens, A and Lash, S (1994) *Reflexive Modernization: Politics, Tradition and Aesthetics in the Modern Social Order* Oxford: Polity Press

Beck, U and Beck-Gernsheim, E (2002) *Individualization* London: Sage

Bernstein, B (1975) *Class, Codes and Control Vol 3.* London: Routledge

Bernstein, B (1996) *Pedagogy, Symbolic Control and Identity: Theory, Research, Critique* London: Taylor and Francis

Bettie, J (2003) *Women without Class: Girls, Race and Identity* Berkeley: University of California Press

Bird, J. (1996) *Black Students and Higher Education.* Buckingham: Open University Press/SRHE

Blackburn, R and Jarman, J (1993) Changing Inequalities in Access to British Universities *Oxford Review of Education* 19: 2, p197-215

Blanden, J and S Machin (2003) *Educational Inequality and the Expansion of UK Higher Education*, Centre for Economic Performance mimeo. London School of Economics

Bonnett, A and Carrington, B. (2000). Fitting into Categories or Falling between them? Rethinking ethnic classifications. *British Journal of Sociology of Education*, 21: 4, p487-500

Bottero, W and Irwin, S (2003) Locating difference: class, 'race' and gender, and the shaping of social inequalities *Sociological Review* 51: 4, p463-483

Bourdieu, P (1967) Systems of education and systems of thought *Social Science Information*, 14, p338-58

Bourdieu, P (1977) Cultural Reproduction and Social Reproduction, in J. Karabel and A H Halsey (eds) *Power and Ideology in Education* New York: Oxford University Press

Bourdieu, P (1983) The field of cultural production or the economic world reversed *Poetics* 12, p311-356

Bourdieu, P (1984) *Distinction*. London: Routledge and Kegan Paul

Bourdieu, P (1985a) The genesis of the concepts of Habitus and of Field *Sociocriticism* 2, p11-24

Bourdieu, P (1985b) From Rules to Strategies: An interview with Pierre Bourdieu *Cultural Anthropology* 1, p110-120.

Bourdieu, P (1986) The Forms of Capital in J G Robinson (ed) *Handbook of Theory and Research for the Sociology of Education* New York: Greenwood Press

Bourdieu, P (1988) *Homo Academicus* Cambridge: Polity Press

Bourdieu, P (1990a) *The Logic of Practice* Cambridge: Polity Press

Bourdieu, P (1990b) *In Other words: Essays towards a reflexive sociology* Cambridge: Polity Press

Bourdieu, P (1993) *Sociology in Question* London: Sage.

Bourdieu, P (1998) *Practical Reason* Cambridge: Polity Press

Bourdieu, P (1999) The Contradictions of Inheritance in Bourdieu, P and A Accardo, G Balazs, S Beaud, F Bonvin, E Bourdieu, P Bourgois, S Broccolichi, P Champagne, R Christin, J-P Faguer, S Garcia, R Lenoir, F Oeuvrard, M Pialoux, L Pinto, D Podalydes, A Sayad, C Soulie, L J D Wacquant *Weight of the World: Social suffering in contemporary society* Cambridge: Polity Press

Bourdieu, P and Passeron, J C (1977) *Reproduction in Education, Society and Culture* London: Sage

Bourdieu, P and Passeron, J C (1979) *The Inheritors: French Students and their Relation to Culture* Chicago: University of Chicago Press

Bourdieu, P and Wacquant, L (1992) *An Invitation to Reflexive Sociology* Chicago: University of Chicago Press

Bourdieu, P and Maluiiski, L (2000) Changes in social structure and changes in the demand for education, in S J Ball (ed) *Sociology of Education: Major Themes, Volume 2, Inequalities and Oppressions* London, RoutledgeFalmer

Boyle, RP (1966) The Effect of High School on Student Aspirations *American Journal of Sociology* 72, p628-639

Breen, R. and Goldthorpe, J H (1997) Explaining Educational Differentials: Towards a Formal Rational Action Theory *Rationality and Society* 9: 3, p275-305

Bridge, G (2001) Bourdieu, rational action and the time-space strategy of gentrification *Transactions of the Institute of British Geographers* 26, p205-224

Brierley, S (1995) *The Advertising Handbook* London: Routledge

Brooks, R (2002) 'Edinburgh, Exeter, East London – or employment?' A review of research on young people's higher education choices *Educational Research* 44: 2, p217-227

Brooks, R (2004) 'My mum would be as pleased as punch if I actually went, but my dad seems a bit more particular about it': paternal involvement in young people's higher education choices *British Educational Research Journal* 30: 4, p495-514

Brooks, R (2005) *Friendship and Educational Choice* London: Palgrave Macmillan

Brown, P (1996) Cultural Capital and Social Exclusion: Some observations on recent trends in education, employment and the labour market *Work, Employment and Society* 9:1, p29-52

Brynner, J, Ferri, E and Shepherd, P (1997) *Twenty-Something in the 1990s: getting on, getting by, getting nowhere* Aldershot: Ashgate

Burke, P J (2002) *Accessing Education: effectively widening participation* Stoke-on-Trent: Trentham Books

Butler,T (1997) *Gentrification and the middle classes* Aldershot: Ashgate

Butler, T and Savage, M (eds) (1995) *Social change and the middle classes* London: UCL Press

Callender, C (2003a) *Attitudes to Debt: School leavers and further education students' attitudes to debt and their impact on participation in higher education* London: Universities UK

Callender, C (2003b) 'Student Financial Support in Higher Education: Access and Exclusion', in M Tight (ed) *Access and Exclusion: International Perspectives on Higher Education Research* London: Elsevier Science

Callender, C and Kemp, M (2000) Changing Student Finances: Income, Expenditure and the Take-up of Student Loans Among Full- and Part-time Higher Education Students in 1998-9, *DfEE Research Report* 213, DfEE, Nottingham

Castells, M (1997) *The Power of Identity* London: Blackwell

Cheng, Y (1995) Staying on in Full-Time Education after 16: Do Schools Make a Difference? *DfEE Research Series Youth Cohort Report No 37*

Chevalier, A and Conlon, G (2004) *Does it pay to attend a prestigious university? CEE Discussion paper* London: Centre for the Economics of Education, LSE

Chisholm, L (1995) Cultural Semantics, occupations and gender discourse in P Atkinson, B Davies and S Delamont (eds) *Discourse and Reproduction* Creskill, NJ: Hampton Press

Cicourel, A (1993) Aspects of Structural and Processual Theories of Knowledge in Calhoun, C, E LiPuma and M Postone (eds) Bourdieu: *Critical Perspectives* Cambridge: Polity Press

Coffield, F and Vignoles, A (1997) *Widening Participation to Higher Education by Gender, Ethnicity and Age* Report 5 of the National Committee of Inquiry into Higher Education

Collins, J (1999) Introduction *Qualitative Studies in Education: Special Issue on Higher Education* 12: 3, p229-237

Cook, J (2000) Culture, Class and Taste in S Munt (ed) *Cultural Studies and the Working class: Subject to Change* London: Cassell

Connor, H, Burton, Pearson, R, Pollard, E and Regan, J (1999) *Making the Right Choice: How Students Choose Universities and Colleges London:* CVCP

Connor, H,Tyers, C, Modood,T and Hillage, J (2004) Why the Difference? A Closer Look at Higher Education *Minority Ethnic Students and Graduates Research Report 552* Nottingham: DfES

Cote, J E (1996) Sociological perspectives on identity formation: the culture identity link and identity capital *Journal of Adolescence* 19, p417-428

CRE (Commission for Racial Equality) (1999) *Ethnicities in Britain: CRE Bulletin* London: Commission for Racial Equality

David, M E (2004) Feminist Sociology and Feminist Knowledges: Contributions to Higher Education Pedagogies and Professional Practices in the Knowledge Economy *International Studies in the Sociology of Education* 14 (2) p99-123

David, M E (2003) *Personal and Political: Feminisms, Sociology and Family Lives*, Stoke-on-Trent: Trentham Books

David, M E (2003) Minding the Gaps between Family, Home and School: Pushy or Pressurised Mummies? in Castelli, S, M, Mendel and B, Ravn (eds) *School, Family and Community Partnership in a World of Differences and Changes* (Wydawnictwo Uniwersytetu Gdanskiego, Gdansk, Poland) proceedings of the European Research Network for Parents and Education (ERNAPE) conference held in Gdansk, Poland, September 4th-6th

David M E (1993) *Parents, Gender and Education Reform*, Cambridge, Polity Press

David, M E, D Reay, J Davies, S J Ball (2003) Gender Issues in Parental Involvement in Student Choices of Higher Education *Gender and Education*, 15: 1, p21- 3

David, M E, A West and J Ribbens, (1994) *Mother's Intuition? Choosing Secondary Schools* London, Falmer

David, M E, J Davies, R Edwards, D. Reay and K Standing (1996) Mothering and Education: reflexivity and feminist methodology in L Morley and V Walsh (eds) *Breaking Boundaries: Women in Higher Education* London: Taylor and Francis

Devine, D (2004) *Children, Power and Schooling* Stoke-on-Trent: Trentham Books

Devine, F (2004) *Class Practices: how parents help their children get good jobs* Cambridge: Cambridge University Press

DfES (2003) *The level of highest qualification held by young people and adults* London: Department for Education and Skills

Di Maggio, P (1979) Review Essay on Pierre Bourdieu *American Journal of Sociology* 84, p1460-74

Douglas, M (1975) *Implicit Meanings* London: Routledge

Du Bois-Reymond, M (1998) 'I Don't Want to Commit Myself Yet': Young People's Life Concepts, *Journal of Youth Studies* 1:1, p63-79.

Dumais, S (2002) Cultural Capital, Gender, and School Success: The Role of Habitus *Sociology of Education* 75, p44-68

Duru-Bellat, M (2000) Social inequalities in the French education system: the joint effect of individual and contextual factors, *Journal of Education Policy* 15: 1, p33-40

Egerton, M. (1999) Monitoring Contemporary Student Flows and Characteristics: secondary analyses using the Labour Force Survey and the General Household Survey University of Manchester, unpublished paper

Egerton, M and Halsey, A H (1993) Trends by Social Class and Gender in access to Higher Education in Britain *Oxford Review of Education* 19: 2, p183-196

Falsey, B and Heigns, B (1984) The College Channel: Private and Public School reconsidered *Sociology of Education* 57, p111-122

Farnell, B (2000) Getting out of the Habitus: An alternative model of dynamically embodied social action *Journal of the Royal Anthropological Institute* 6, p397-418

Freeborn, C (2000) 'Now or Never' *Guardian Education* 3 October, p10-11

Foskett, N and Hemsley-Brown, J (2001) *Choosing Futures: young people's decision making in education, training and career markets* London: Routledge Falmer

Furlong, A and Cartmel, F (1997) *Young People and Social Change: individualisation and risk in late modernity* Buckingham: Open University Press

Galindo-Rueda, F and Vignoles, A F (2002) Class Ridden or Meritocratic? An Economic Analysis of Recent Changes in Britain *IZA Discussion Paper* No. 677

Galindo-Rueda, F, Vignoles, A F and Marcenaro-Gutier, O (2004) *The Widening Socio-economic Gap in UK* Higher Education Centre for the Economics of Education Discussion Paper, London School of Economics

Gambetta, D (1987) *Were they Pushed or did they Jump?* Cambridge: Cambridge University Press

Ganzeboom, H B G, De Graaf, P M and Robert, P (1990) Reproduction Theory on Socialist Ground: Intergenerational Transmission of Inequalities in Hungary in A L Kalleberg, (ed) *Research in Social Stratification and Mobility* vol. 8. Greenwich, CT: JAI Press

Ganzeboom, H B G and Treiman, D J (1991) Educational Expansion and Educational Achievement in Comparative Perspective Paper presented at International Sociological Association Conference Ohio State University USA

Gewirtz, S, Ball, S J and Bowe, R (1995) *Markets, Choice and Education* Milton Keynes: Open University Press

Gillborn, D (1995) Racism, Identity and Modernity: pluralism, moral anti-racism and plastic ethnicity International Studies in the *Sociology of Education*, 5: 1, p1-17

Gillon, E (1999) Accessing Access *AUT Bulletin* January

Glass, D V (1954) *Social Mobility in Britain* London: Routledge and Kegan Paul

Goldthorpe, J (1995) The Service Class Revisited in T Butler and M Savage (eds) *Social Change and the Middle Classes* London: UCL Press

Goldthorpe, J (1998) Rational Action Theory for Sociology *British Journal of Sociology* 49: 2, p167-92

Grenfell, M (2003) Bourdieu in the Classroom in M Olssen (ed) *Culture and Learning: Access and Opportunity in the Curriculum* Westport: Greenwood Press

Grenfell, M and James, D (1998) (eds) *Bourdieu and Education: Acts of Practical Theory* London: Falmer

Hagerstrand, T (1975) Survival and arena: on the life history of individuals in relation to their geographical environment in T Carlstein, D Parkes and M Thrift (eds) *Human Activity and Time Geography* London: Edward Arnold

Halsey, A H (1993) Trends in access and equity in higher education: Britain in international perspective *Oxford Review of Education* 19: 2, p129-40

Halsey, A H, Heath, A and Ridge, J (1980) *Origins and Destinations: family, class and education in modern Britain* Oxford: Clarendon

Hartmann, M (2000) Class-specific habitus and the social reproduction of the business elite in Germany and France *Sociological Review* 48, p241- 261

Harvey, D (1989) *The Condition of Postmodernity* Oxford: Basil Blackwell

Hatcher, R (1998) Class Differentiation in Education: rational choices? *British Journal of Sociology of Education* 19:1, p5-24

Heidegger, M (1962) *Being and Time* New York: Harper and Row

Hill, P (2004) Class gap widens under Blair *Times Higher Education Supplement* July 2 2004, p1

Hesketh, A J (1999) Towards an economic sociology of the student financial experience of higher education *Journal of Education Policy* 14:4, p385-410

Holdsworth, C (2005, forthcoming) 'Don't you think you're missing out living at home?' student experiences and residential transitions *Sociological Review*

James, D (1995) Mature Studentship in Higher Education: beyond a 'species' approach *British Journal of Sociology of Education* 16, p451-466

James, D (1996) The Home and the University: Habitus and diversity of experience in studentship. Paper presented at the BERA conference, September 1996 Lancaster University

Jamieson, K. H. (1984) *Packaging the Presidency: Presidential Campaign Advertising,* New York: Oxford University Press

Jenkins, R. (1992) *Pierre Bourdieu* London. Routledge

Kastillis, J and Rubinson, R (1990) Cultural Resources and School Success: Gender, Ethnicity, and Poverty Groups within an Urban School District. *American Sociological Review,* 55, p127-142

Kirton, A (1999) Lessons from Access Education in A Hayton (ed) *Tackling Disaffection and Social Exclusion* London: Kogan Page

Lampl, P (2004) Imbalance of Talent *Times Higher Education Supplement* August 20 2004, p16

Lareau, A (1989) *Home Advantage* London: Falmer

Lareau, A (2004) *Unequal Childhoods: Class, Race, and Family Life* Berkeley: University of California Press

Lareau, A and Weininger, E (2003) Cultural Capital in Educational Research: A Critical Assessment *Theory and Society* 32: 5-6, p567-606

Lauder, H, Hughes, D, Watson, S, Waslander, S, Thrupp, M, Strathdee, R, Simiyu, I, Dupuis, A, McGlinn, J, and Hamlin, J (1999) *Trading in Futures: Why Markets in Education Don't Work* Buckingham: Open University Press

Lawler, S (2000) *Mothering the Self: mothers, daughters, subjects* London: Routledge

Maguire, M, Ball, S J and Macrae, S (2000) 'In the house and givin' it large': Young women, feminism and 'choices' in the new millennium' Unpublished paper Department of Education King's College London

Maguire, M, Ball, S J and Macrae, S. (1999) Promotion, Persuasion and Class-taste: Marketing (in) the UK post compulsory sector *British Journal of Sociology of Education* 20: 3, p291-308

Mason, D (2000) *Race and Ethnicity in Modern Britain.* (2nd ed.). Oxford: Oxford University Press

McDonough, P (1997) *Choosing Colleges: How Social Class and Schools Structure Opportunity* New York: State University of New York Press

McNamara Horvat, E and Lising, A A (1999) 'Hey, Those Shoes are out of Uniform': African American Girls in an Elite School and the Importance of Habitus *Anthropology and Education Quarterly* 30,

Metcalf, H (1997) *Class and Higher Education: the participation of young people from lower social classes* London: Policy Studies Institute/CIHE

Mirza, H (1995) Black women in higher education: defining a space/finding a place in L Morley and V Walsh (eds) *Feminist Academics: creative agents for change* London: Taylor and Francis

Modood, T (2003) Ethnic Differentials in Educational Performance in Mason, D (ed) *Explaining Ethnic Differences* ESRC and The Policy Press

Modood, T and Acland, T (1998) (eds) *Race and Higher Education Report 841* London: Policy Studies Institute

Modood, T, Beiston, Sand Virdee, S. (1994) *Changing Ethnic Identities* London: Policy Studies Institute

Modood, T and Shiner, M (1994) *Ethnic Minorities and Higher Education:Why are there differential rates of entry?* London: Policy Studies Institute

Mohr, J, and DiMaggio, P (1995) The Intergenerational Transmission of Cultural Capital p167-199 in *Research in Social Stratification and Mobility,* Vol 14 Greenwich, CT: JAI Press

Moogan, Y J, Baron, S and Harris, K (1999) Decision making behaviour of potential higher education students *Higher Education Quarterly* 53: 3, p211-228

Nash, R (1999) Realism in the Sociology of Education: 'explaining' social differences in attainment *British Journal of Sociology of Education* 20: 1, p107-25

OECD (1998) *Economics and Finance of Lifelong Learning* Paris: Organisation for Economic Co-operation and Development

O'Leary, J (2000) Demand on the decline *The Times* April 14 Section 2 page 13

ONS (Office for National Statistics) (2001) *ONS Census Bulletin 2001* London: Office for National Statistics

Osler, A (1999). The Educational Experiences and Career Aspirations of Black and Ethnic Minority Undergraduates. *Race, Ethnicity and Education* 2: 1, p39-58

Ozga, J and Sukhnandan, L (1998) Undergraduate Non-Completion: Developing an Explanatory Model *Higher Education Quarterly* 52: 3, p316-333

Pajackowska, C and Young, L (1992) Race, representation and psychoanalysis in J Donald and A Rattansi (eds) *Race, Culture, Difference* London: Sage

Parkin, F (1974) Strategies of social closure in class formation, in: F Parkin (ed) *The Social Analysis of Class Structure* London: Tavistock

Payne, J (2003) The Impact of Part-time Jobs in Years 12 and 13 on Qualification Achievement *British Educational Research Journal* 29: 4, p599-610

Plummer , G (2000) *Failing Working Class Girls* Stoke on Trent: Trentham Books

Power, S, Edwards, T, Whitty, G and Wignall, V (2003) *Education and the Middle Class* Buckingham: Open University Press

Pugsley, L (1998) 'Throwing your brains at it: higher education, markets and choice' *International Studies in Sociology of Education* 8: 1, p71-90

Purcell, K (2002) *Qualifications and Careers: Equal opportunities and earning among graduates* Manchester, EOC: Working Paper Series 1

Reay, D (1997) The double-bind of the 'working class' feminist academic: The success of failure or the failure of success in P Mahony and C Zmroczek (eds) *Class Matters: 'Working class' Women's Perspectives on Social Class* London: Taylor and Francis

Reay, D (1998a)'Always Knowing' and 'Never being sure': Institutional and familial habituses and higher education choice *Journal of Education Policy* 13: 4, p519-529

Reay, D (1998b) *Class Work: Mothers' involvement in their children's primary schooling* London: University College Press

Reay, D (2000) A useful extension of Bourdieu's conceptual framework?: Emotional capital as a way of understanding mothers' involvement in children's schooling *Sociological Review* 48: 4, p568-585

Reay, D (2004) 'It's all becoming a habitus'; Beyond the habitual use of habitus in educational research *Special Issue of British Journal of Sociology of Education on Pierre Bourdieu* 25: 4, p431-444

Reay, D (2005, forthcoming) Emotional capital, women and social class in L Adkins and B Skeggs (ed) *Feminism after Bourdieu* Oxford: Blackwell

Reay, D and Ball, S J (1997) 'Spoilt for choice': The working classes and education markets *Oxford Review of Education* 23:1, p89-101

Reay, D and Ball, S J (1998) 'Making their minds up': Family dynamics of school choice' *British Educational Research Journal* 24: 4, p431-448

Reay, D, Ball, S J, David, M E and Davies, J (2001a) Choices of degree or degrees of choice? Social class, race and the higher education choice process *Sociology* 35: 4, p855-874

Reay, D, Ball, S J, David, M E (2001b) Making a Difference?: Institutional habituses and Higher Education Choice *Sociological Research Online* vol 5 no 4 U126-U142.

Reay, D, Ball, S J, and David, M E (2002) 'It's taking me a long time but I'll get there in the end': Mature students on access courses and higher education choice *British Education Research Journal* 28: 1, p5-19

Ricoeur, P (1980) Narrative and Time *Critical Inquiry* 7:1, p169-190

Ricoeur, P (1990) Narrative Identity in D Wood (ed) *Paul Ricoeur: Narrative and Interpretation* London: Routledge

Robbins, L (1963) *Higher Education: Report of a Committee Cmnd 2154* London: HMSO

Robbins, D (1991) *The Work of Pierre Bourdieu: Recognising Society* Milton Keynes: Open University Press

Roberts, K (1993) Career trajectories and the mirage of increased social mobility in I Bates and G Riseborough (eds) *Youth and Inequality* Buckingham: Open University Press

Roker, D (1993) Gaining an edge: girls at a private school in I Bates and G Riseborough (eds) *Youth and Inequality* (p122-138) Buckingham: Open University Press

Rose, N (1998) *Inventing Our Selves: psychology, power and personhood* Cambridge: Cambridge University Press

Rudd, P and Evans, K (1998) Structure and Agency in Youth Transitions: Student Experiences of Vocational Further Education *Journal of Youth Studies* 1: 1, p39-62

Rupp, J C C and De Lange, R (1989) Social Order, Cultural Capital and Citizenship: An essay concerning educational status and educational power versus comprehensiveness of elementary schools *Sociological Review* 37: 4, p668-705

Savage, M (2000) *Class Analysis and Social Transformation* Buckingham: Open University Press

Savage, M (2003) A New Class Paradigm? Review Article *British Journal of Sociology of Education* 24: 4, p535-541

Savage, M, Barlow, J, Dickens, P and Fielding, T (1992) *Property, Bureaucracy and Culture: Middle Class Formation in Contemporary Britain* London: Routledge

Savage, M, Bagnall, G and Longhurst, B (2001) Ordinary, ambivalent and defensive: class identities in the northwest of England *Sociology* 35; 4, p875-892

Sawchuk, P (2003) *Adult Learning and Technology in Working Class Life* Cambridge: Cambridge University Press

Schneider, B and Stevenson, D (1999) *The Ambitious Generation: America's Teenagers, Motivated but Directionless* New Haven: Yale University Press

Shilling, C (2004) Physical Capital and Situated Action: A New Direction for Corporeal Sociology *British Journal of Sociology of Education Special Issue on the Sociology of Pierre Bourdieu* 25: 4, p473-488

Shils, E A, and Finch, H A (1949) *Max Weber on the Methodology of the Social Sciences* Glencoe: Ill: The Free Press

Shiner, M and Modood, T (2002) Help or Hindrance? Higher Education and the Route to Ethnic Equality *British Journal of Sociology of Education* 23: 2, p209-232

Shumar, W (1997) *College for Sale: A critique of the commodification of higher education* London: Falmer

Silva, E (2004) Conceptions of home and family in cultural capital theory Paper presented at the Cultural Capital and Social Exclusion Symposium, Hughs College, Oxford University January 2004

Skeggs, B (1997) *Formations of Class and Gender* London: Sage

Skeggs, B (2004) *Class, Self, Culture* London: Routledge

Smith, D and Tomlinson, S (1989) *The School Effect: A Study of Multi-racial Comprehensives* London: Institute of Policy Studies

Smithers, R (2000) Third of Oxford colleges still take more independent school pupils *The Guardian* August 5 p4

Smithers, A and Robinson, P (1995) *Post-18 Education. Growth, Change, Prospect* London: CIHE

Spivak, G C (1993) Can the Subaltern Speak? in Williams, P and Chrisman, L (eds) *Colonial Discourse and Post-Colonial Theory* Hemel Hempstead: Wheatsheaf Harvester

Strauss, A L (1987) *Qualitative Data Analysis* New York: Cambridge University Press

Sullivan, A (2001) Cultural Capital and Educational Attainment. *Sociology* 35, p893-912

Taylor, C (1992) *The Ethics of Authenticity* Cambridge, Massachusettes: Harvard University Press

Taylor, P (1992). Ethnic Group data and applications to higher education. *Higher Education Quarterly*, 46: 4, p359-374

Thompson, E. P (1968) *The Making of the English Working class* Harmondsworth: Penguin

Tomlinson, S (2001) *Education in a Post-welfare Society* Buckingham: Open University Press

Thrupp, M (1999) *Schools Making a Difference: Let's be realistic!* Buckingham: Open University Press

Tysome, T (2004) Sector caught in parent trap *Times Higher Educational Supplement* 30 July 2004, p1

UCAS (2000) *Statistical Bulletin on Widening Participation* Cheltenham: UCAS

Universities UK (2002) *Social Class and Participation: Good practice in widening access to higher education*, UUK/HECE/SCOP London

Vincent, C, Ball, S J and Kemp, S (2004) The social geography of childcare: making up a middle class child *British Journal of Sociology of Education* 25: 2, p229-244

Wakeford, N (1993) Beyond educating Rita: mature students and Access courses *Oxford Review of Education* 19: 2, p217-30

Wacquant, L (1991) Towards a Reflexive Sociology: A workshop with Pierre Bourdieu *Sociological Theory* 7, p26-63

Walkerdine, V, Lucey, H and Melody, J (2001) *Growing up Girl: Psychosocial Explorations of Gender and Class* London: Palgrave

Weick, K (1976) Educational Organisations as Loosely Coupled Systems *Administrative Science Quarterly* 21, p1-19

West, A, Noden, P, Edge, A, David, M E and Davies, J (1998) 'Choices and Expectations at the primary and secondary stages in the state and private sectors, *Educational Studies*, 24: 1, p45-60.

Weininger, E (2004) Foundations of Pierre Bourdieu's Class Analysis in E Olin Wright (ed) *Approaches to Class Analysis* Cambridge: Cambridge University Press

Woodward, W. (2000) Britain tops US in degree league *The Guardian* May 17 p5

Author Index

Subject Index